The North American Martyrs

The North American Martyrs

Jesuits in the New World

by Lillian M. Fisher

Pauline
BOOKS & MEDIA
Boston

Library of Congress Cataloging-in-Publication Data

Fisher, Lillian M.
  The North American martyrs : Jesuits in the New World / Lillian M. Fisher.
  p. cm.
  Includes bibliographical references.
  ISBN 0-8198-5132-9 (paper)
  1. Christian saints — New France — Biography.   2. Christian martyrs — New France — Biography.   3. Jesuits — New France — Biography.   4. New France — Church history.   5. Jesuits —Missions — New France.   6. Missionaries — France — Biography.   7. Missionaries — New France — Biography.   I. Title.
  BX3755.F57 1996
  272' .9'0971— dc20
                                                                    0120418
                                                                    CIP

ISBN 0-8198-5132-9

Printed and published in the U.S.A. by Pauline Books & Media, 50 Saint Pauls Avenue, Boston MA 02130-3491.

www.pauline.org

Pauline Books & Media is the publishing house of the Daughters of St. Paul, an international congregation of women religious serving the Church with the communications media.

1 2 3 4 5 6 7   06 05 04 03 02 01

Contents

Editor's note

The eight Jesuit martyrs who came from France to evangelize in the New World saw their encounter with the native peoples as an opportunity to bring the Gospel of Jesus Christ to those who had never heard it. Although in many ways the Jesuits sought to accommodate themselves to the native culture, their understanding of inculturation was different from how the Church views it today. The pastoral letter from the Canadian bishops included in this volume deals with some aspects of this important and sensitive issue.

The Jesuit Relations are the primary source for the historical information in this book. The various quotations that appear are taken from the *Relations* and rendered in more current English. Because this volume is intended as a biography to inspire its readers and not as a scholarly work, footnotes were not added to the various quotations in order not to burden the text.

INTRODUCTION

In the early seventeenth century, eight courageous French-men sailed to Quebec to bring the Gospel to a new world. Even if they had known what awaited them, they would not have turned back. They were Jesuits. True sons of St. Ignatius Loyola, they had the strength of character and determination to face whatever would come, just as their founder overcame incredible obstacles to establish a religious order that has endured even to this day.

The Jesuit missionaries were going to evangelize the native peoples living in New France, which comprised eastern Canada and Ontario and extended into Maine and New York State. In 1534, the Frenchman Jacques Cartier had sailed into the great bay of an enormous river and named it after St. Lawrence. As he sailed 100 miles upstream, he came to a giant bluff that rose 300 feet into the sky. Cartier climbed the cliff, planted the French flag on the top, and claimed the land for France. Impressed with the enormous size of the cliff, he reportedly said in his Norman dialect, "Que-bec!"—"what a rock!"

For the next seventy years, however, the French did not take any significant steps to colonize the area. But in 1603, King Henry IV of France bestowed a charter on the Company of Merchants, mainly Calvinist businessmen, which enabled them to explore and exploit the resources of New France, or

Canada. The chief explorer in the Company, Samuel de Champlain, was a Catholic who had served the king of France and had extensive experience in leading expeditions. In 1603 and 1604, Champlain surveyed the Atlantic Coast from Cape Cod to the St. Lawrence River, and discovered an island that he named Mont Real (Montreal). In 1608, Champlain made his third trip to New France. He began a settlement at Quebec, traveled to what is now New York State, and discovered Lake Champlain.

Back in Europe, the Thirty Years' War (1618–1648) which was soon to break out, would bring the British and the French into conflict. The hostility and suspicion bred by war extended even to the New World, and the French settlers were uneasy about the Dutch settlers along the Hudson. The British and the Dutch wanted to prevent French expansion and were prepared to do so at any cost.

Other conflicts involved the native peoples. The Algonquins claimed land along the St. Lawrence River and the New England coast. The Hurons made their home along Lake Huron and the Iroquois inhabited areas of what is now New York State. For years there had been fighting among the three nations, and tensions only increased with the arrival of the Europeans.

The Algonquins along the St. Lawrence River made friends with the French, mainly for trading purposes. In New York State, the Iroquois traded amicably with the Dutch, but the rapport was fragile and unpredictable. In 1609, an event would occur that would shape the Iroquois' attitude toward the French for many years.

Champlain traveled west to Huron country, accompanied by Algonquin warriors who knew the land, the wilderness, and how to survive in it. The expedition came upon a war party of Iroquois at Ticonderoga. The Iroquois were skilled warriors and could easily have defeated the exploration party had it not been for the fact that the French had muskets. After the battle, Champlain continued on to the Huron country, but left behind a band of Iroquois who provoked animosity among their people toward the French.

The first French missionaries to evangelize in the New World were the Franciscan Recollets, who established themselves there in 1615. But the conditions of the colony proved very demanding, and they eventually asked the Jesuits for assistance. In 1625 the Jesuits received permission to begin a mission in New France, and the first three Jesuit priests were sent.

Thus began the great Jesuit missionary effort in the New World. Faced with the formidable challenges of encountering a new culture, learning new languages, and enduring the harsh climate, and more, these dedicated priests suffered hardships of every kind, unspeakable indignities, and the ultimate sacrifice: martyrdom. Today we honor these martyrs as Saints Jean de Brébeuf, Isaac Jogues, Gabriel Lalemant, Antoine Daniel, Charles Garnier, René Goupil, Jean de la Lande, and Noël Chabanel. This is their story.

CHRONOLOGY OF THE MARTYRS

St. John de Brébeuf

Born March 25, 1593, at Condé-sur-Vire, Normandy, France

Entered the Jesuits October 5, 1617

Arrived in New France 1625

Returned to France 1629

Returned to New France 1633

Martyred at St. Ignace Mission, Ontario, March 16, 1649

Huron name: Echon

St. Noël Chabanel

Born February 7, 1613, at Saugues, France

Entered the Jesuits 1630

Arrived in New France 1643

Martyred near the Nottawasaga River, Ontario,
December 8, 1649

St. Anthony Daniel

Born May 27, 1610 at Dieppe, France

Entered the Jesuits October 1, 1621

Arrived in New France 1632

Martyred at St. Joseph Mission, Ontario, July 4, 1648

Huron name: Antwen

St. Charles Garnier

Born May 25, 1605 at Paris, France

Entered the Jesuits September 26, 1624

Arrived in New France 1636

Martyred at St. Jean Mission, Ontario, December 7, 1649

Huron name: Ouracha

St. René Goupil

Born May 13, 1608 at Anjou, France

Became a *donné* 1640

Martyred at Ossernenon (now Auriesville), New York, 1642

St. Isaac Jogues

Born January 10, 1607 at Orléans, France

Entered the Jesuits October 24, 1624

Arrived in New France 1636

Captured, tortured and held in captivity 1642

Escaped and returned to France 1643

Returned to Canada 1644

Martyred at Ossernenon (now Auriesville), New York, October 18, 1646

Huron name: Ondessonk

St. Gabriel Lalemant

Born October 31, 1610 at Paris, France

Entered the Jesuits on March 24, 1630

Arrived in New France 1646

Martyred at St. Ignace Mission, Ontario, March 17, 1649

Huron name: Atironta

St. Jean de la Lande

Born in Dieppe, France

Became a *donné* 1642 ?

Martyred at Ossernenon (now Auriesville), New York, October 19, 1646

CHAPTER ONE

Jean de Brébeuf, a young Jesuit priest, wondered if a letter would ever come. Ever since he had met the two Franciscan Recollets, Father Ireneé Piat and Brother Gabriel Sagard-Theodat, who had returned from the Canadian missions, a great desire had stirred in his heart to preach the Gospel in the New World. De Brébeuf informed his new provincial, Father Coton, that he wanted to volunteer for the missions in Quebec. But de Brébeuf had suffered a number of illnesses and it was unlikely that he would be sent to such a demanding mission field. Yet, nothing seemed to dampen the young Jesuit's persistence. He pleaded for Father Coton's permission to go to Canada, if not immediately, at least in the future. While he waited for word, de Brébeuf carried out his duties as bursar for the Jesuit College at Rouen.

When the long-awaited letter finally arrived, de Brébeuf held his breath as he opened it. He scanned its contents and shouted a prayer of thanksgiving. He was to accompany Father Charles Lalemant, Father Ennemond Massé, and the lay brothers Frère François Charton and Frère Gilbert Burel to New France! De Brébeuf had desired this assignment so intensely that he had hardly allowed himself to dream about it. Now he found it hard to believe that he would actually be setting sail the following month.

For the next few weeks, the priests and brothers kept incredibly busy writing letters, notifying relatives, and putting business affairs in order. They had to purchase warm clothing, boots, gloves, cloaks, and other items suited to Canada's cold climate. They packed tools, building materials, and household supplies. Since virtually nothing could be purchased in Quebec and new supplies arrived only in summer, they would also take medicines, books, trading goods, and everything necessary to celebrate Mass.

The priests and lay brothers boarded three small ships on Wednesday, April 23, 1625, and waited for a favorable tide and wind. The next day the commander gave the order for the ships to set sail from Dieppe. De Brébeuf leaned over the ship's rail and watched the shores of his beloved France fade from view as the vessel moved farther out into the ocean. He was finally on his way to the missions in Quebec. Although he had left behind everything he cherished, de Brébeuf had never been happier. He had surrendered all to God.

The small ships carrying the band of missionaries reached the southern corridor of the St. Lawrence River in the first week of June. Drawing closer to Quebec, the three ships dropped anchors and sails and awaited favorable weather conditions that would allow them to move into the harbor of Tadoussac. De Brébeuf took in the sight from the deck. The salt air that had pervaded everything for the past seven weeks gave way to a welcome scent of fragrant pine trees. Bark canoes paddled by men with reddish brown skin that glowed in the fading sunlight could be seen skimming the water gracefully. When night fell, fires gleamed through the branches of giant trees along the shores. This new, mysterious, and beautiful world stirred de Brébeuf's heart and he thanked God for allowing him to come.

The next morning he woke to a glorious day as the ship floated gently into the harbor of Tadoussac. A wide sandy beach led to the tree line and the hills and gray rocks that seemed to climb to the heavens. Everywhere de Brébeuf looked, there were native men, women, and children scurrying about. The children roamed about naked, while the men wore loincloths, and the women, loose-fitting tunics. The native people appraised the Jesuits and the ship's crew warily.

The native men spoke in guttural tones, unlike anything de Brébeuf had ever heard. Some of them had decorated their faces and bodies with white, blue, red, and black paint. The sight fascinated Father de Brébeuf, and the native people seemed just as curious about him and the other Jesuits. They were familiar with the Recollets' garb of coarse gray robes, sandals, and white belts, but the Jesuits wore black from head to toe, strange large-brimmed hats, and their thick beards that hid their mouths and chins. The beads that hung from the strangers' waists puzzled them as well. They viewed the Jesuits cautiously. Who were these intruders? What did they want?

The three French ships remained docked at Tadoussac all summer, but smaller crafts carried freight and passengers, including Jean de Brébeuf and the others, farther up the St. Lawrence River. They traveled slowly through the swirling waters and sighted the massive rock known as Quebec on the fifth day of their journey. They docked their small boats beneath the wall of the rock on June 15—fifty-two days since the Jesuits had set sail from Dieppe.

They looked with curiosity at the town from the boat. Although the colony of Quebec had been founded seventeen years earlier, it had fewer than 100 inhabitants. The seven French families who had settled there had only six children among them. Having made little progress in agriculture except for the small attempts made by the Recollets, the colony depended entirely on France for its food supplies.

Emery de Caen, Commandant of Quebec in Champlain's absence, came to meet them. He boarded the boat, smiled, and bowed, but then requested letters of introduction—documents giving them permission to enter Quebec—from the Jesuits. Fathers de Brébeuf, Lalemant, and Massé remained speechless. Of course they were authorized to enter Quebec, but they had no documents to prove it. Again, de Caen smiled politely and informed the Jesuits that if they could not produce the necessary documents, they would have to return to France. De Caen turned around and climbed out of the boat, leaving the surprised Jesuits behind. They turned to each other and asked, "What can we do now?" De Brébeuf paced restlessly up and down the deck as he considered their predicament.

When the Recollet superior, Father Joseph Le Caron, learned what had happened, he hurried to meet the Jesuits and greeted them cordially. He then went to speak with Commandant de Caen, who protested that the Jesuits had no place to stay. Le Caron assured de Caen that the Recollets would shelter them and, after arguing for a while, de Caen finally agreed.

Although the Recollet Fathers had cramped living quarters, they warmly welcomed the Jesuits and invited them to stay as long as they wished. The Recollets gladly shared what little they had of their own supplies, which allowed the Jesuits to be independent of the Montmorency Company, a group of mostly Calvinist merchants who used Quebec as a summer trading post. The company shipped furs and other local goods to France and made exorbitant profits while exploiting the native peoples.

Sharing their experience of New France, the Recollets detailed the difficulties they had encountered in their missionary efforts. They had baptized only a few Algonquins and Montagnais who came to trade at Quebec. Since they were an itinerant people, it was almost impossible to learn their language in order to be able to catechize them. However, Le Caron spoke of the Hurons as a people he thought would be receptive to Christianity, and de Brébeuf listened with deep interest.

Two weeks later, de Brébeuf and Daillon sailed up the St. Lawrence River to seek passage to the Huron country. They took along the necessary supplies as well as a list of Huron words and phrases that Le Caron and Sagard-Theodat had compiled. After traveling three days, they anchored near Trois Rivières (Three Rivers) and spent a few days there. Then they sailed farther up the river to a Huron trading post. De Brébeuf and Daillon realized that they would be viewed as intruders and that dangers lay ahead. They asked permission to travel in the canoes going back to Huronia, but the native men refused to take them. Sensing that the right moment had not arrived, the priests returned to Quebec.

Undaunted, Father Jean de Brébeuf sought other ways to evangelize. Utilizing his gift for languages, de Brébeuf learned the dialect of the Montagnais and then, in the winter of 1625–1626, joined a hunting party of Montagnais. He treasured the list of native words that Le Caron and Sagard-Theodat had transcribed, which allowed him to communicate with the people.

At the camp, the first order of business was to find a group that would accept him. After presenting gifts of kettles, beads, and knives, de Brébeuf found a family that was willing to take him into their home. They shared their dwelling, hearth, and food. At times, he found it hard to adapt to the Montagnais' lifestyle. Nevertheless, he was determined to learn about the native peoples by living in their own environment. He found the custom of sharing a pot of meat—with people dipping into the common fare—repellent. But in order for him to be accepted and tolerated, de Brébeuf had to do as the others did. If they smoked, he smoked; if they laughed at some vague joke, he laughed; if the group gathered around a pot of cooked eels, each reaching in for his share, he did the same. All the while de Brébeuf was learning more about the people. He discovered that the native peoples of North America respected the qualities of courage and long-suffering. He shivered in the severe winter cold, perspired in the summer heat, and endured incessant insect bites. He persevered through it all and constantly prayed for strength. No doubt, this new way of life, so foreign to him, must have required heroic discipline.

Father Jean de Brébeuf's struggle in the New World can be better appreciated when contrasted against the background of his life in France. On March 25, 1593, de Brébeuf was born into a family of wealthy landowners in eastern Normandy. Very early in life, de Brébeuf displayed a keen interest in higher learning and, at the age of sixteen, he felt drawn to the Society of Jesus. His lineage had destined him to live the comfortable life of a noble gentleman, but he chose to live under the most demanding conditions for the love of God and the people he desired to evangelize.

While de Brébeuf resided with the Montagnais, Father Charles Lalemant, with Champlain's help, began to build a permanent Jesuit home, Notre-Dame-des-Anges, on the St. Charles River. Supplies arrived from France and with them came Fathers Philibert Noyrot and Anne de Nouë, a lay brother, and twenty workmen. One building served as stable, store-house, workshop, and bakery, while another structure became the residence. The buildings were constructed of rough-hewn planks plastered together with mud, and topped with a roof thatched with grass from the nearby meadows.

After de Brébeuf returned from his stay with the Montagnais in the spring of 1626, he and the Jesuits began to look for ways to find passage to the homeland of the Hurons. When a group of canoes laden with rich beaver furs came down from Huronia that summer, Nouë, Daillon, and de Brébeuf asked to accompany the Hurons on their return trip. The natives agreed to take Daillon, the Recollet priest, because they knew him, but they refused to take de Brébeuf and Noüe. They said that de Brébeuf, a giant of a man, would upset their canoes. When the Jesuits offered the Hurons a liberal supply of gifts, they finally agreed to take all three missionaries with them.

The Iroquois, who were warring against the Hurons and the French, had recently attacked settlers in Quebec, and the small party faced the very real danger of an Iroquois assault, as well as the grueling 800-mile journey along the water route. They were often forced to haul their canoes over land when the rough waters prevented passage. The Jesuits helped carry the heavy canoes over the portages. De Brébeuf often carried Noüe's load besides his own, for Noüe was older and did not have the strength to keep up. They carried food, clothing, vestments, candles, altar wine, books, writing tablets, and other essentials.

After a month's journey, the party sailed into Penetanguishene Bay and landed at a village named Otouacha. Then they traveled over a mile inland through forests, and passed small farming areas, thick with pumpkins, beans, maize, and squash. At a village named Toanché they found the cabin that the Recollet priest, Father Viel, had built in 1623. De Brébeuf would reside here for three years under difficult conditions as he labored to make Christ known. He and the other Jesuits would write reports of their progress and send these writings back to France. The reports, known as *Relations*, would eventually comprise seventy-three volumes. The reports, printed and sold in Paris bookstores, became quite popular and helped obtain support for the Jesuit missions.

In the *Relations*, the priests recounted what they learned of the native culture as they tried to adapt themselves to living among the people. The Hurons lived in clusters of longhouses, structures made of two rows of saplings planted in the ground, then bent and fastened at the top to form an arch. The poles were covered with bark, and a small opening was left at the top of the longhouse both to allow smoke to escape and light to enter. Sometimes as many as fifteen to twenty families shared a longhouse. A central fire served as warmth and shelves along the sides of the house as beds. Benches were used as chairs and tables, while the walls and ceilings were used for storing and hanging items. The town of longhouses was walled in by double rows of logs to provided protection against enemy attack.

The Huron Nation had four major clans: the Bear, the Cord, the Deer, and the Rock. While the chiefs from each clan met in council almost daily, in matters of serious consequence a tribal congregation was summoned.

The Hurons believed in an *oki* or a higher spirit, which they called "Aronhia." This *oki* or supreme being dwelled in the heavens where the spirit sun and the spirit stars and moon presided over earthly things. Although the Hurons believed in the divinity of everything in nature, they only offered sacrifices to Aronhia. When evil befell them, they concluded that Aronhia was angry.

While learning about this culture, de Brébeuf, Daillon, and Noüe continued to travel deeper into the interior of the Huron country—what is now the county of Simcoe, Ontario. Lakes Simcoe and Couchiching, the Severn River, and Matchedash Bay lay to the east and north, and Nottawasaga Bay to the west. The Petuns lived across the bay, and the Neutrals occupied the southwest, living in the Niagara and Detroit peninsulas and spreading into Michigan and New York. Other tribes who spoke the Algonquin dialect dwelled in the area surrounding Huronia.

The Neutral country abounded in resources, especially furs and tobacco, but the Hurons barred the Neutrals from passing through their territory. They did however offer to trade Neutral goods to the French. Although other routes were open to the Neutrals, they did not use them; rather, they allowed the Hurons to do their trading.

Daillon traveled into the Neutrals' territory in order to evangelize them. Rumors began spreading that he had come to stop them from using the Huron's as an intermediary in trade. The native people called Daillon a sorcerer, an evil *oki;* then they burned his possessions and threatened to kill him. When de Brébeuf learned of Daillon's plight, he sent two men to bring him back to Toanché. Eventually, Noüe returned to Quebec; Daillon, who had remained at Toanché for a time, departed in 1628; and de Brébeuf was left alone with the Hurons.

During this solitary period, de Brébeuf composed a Huron dictionary and grammar guide and translated the catechism. He ministered to the people and continued to hope for conversions and baptisms. Despite the hardships of this new life, de Brébeuf threw himself into his work and tried to learn all he could about the native people. He looked for every opportunity to tell them about the Gospel. However, early in the summer of 1629, some jarring news arrived from Quebec.

CHAPTER TWO

Problems continued to plague the colonists at Quebec. Although the population had increased slightly, it still depended on the yearly supplies and food from France. When the ships could not make the journey, the people of Quebec suffered. The growing hostilities between the French and the English also threatened the colony. The impending conflict prompted de Brébeuf's superiors to recall him to Quebec. When he read the orders his face fell, but he immediately prepared for the return trip.

The Hurons learned that de Brébeuf was about to leave them and they begged him to stay, calling him by the name they had given him: Echon. Accustomed to his presence and strange manners, some now regarded him as a friend. De Brébeuf fumbled for words to explain that he had to obey, and said goodbye to his friends, wondering if he would ever see them again. He packed his few belongings and left the chapel in readiness for the day when he would return. He stood on the shore and took one last look at the mission, then got into the canoe to begin the arduous journey. Upon arriving in Quebec, he found the colonists disturbed and excited over a rumor that an English fleet was fast approaching.

A year earlier, in July 1628, David Kirke, the British commander, had issued an ultimatum demanding that Champlain
surrender Quebec. Champlain refused. He tried to bluff the
British commander into believing that Quebec was well sup-
plied with food and arms, although the people were starving.
For now, at least, it appeared that the bluff had worked. But
Kirke soon encountered four small French vessels and out-
fought them, destroying food and other supplies intended for
the colonists. Then he returned to England, planning to return
the following summer with more arms to capture Quebec.

Desperately the inhabitants of Quebec searched the hori-
zon for the French supply ships; their meager rations of peas,
corn, and eels barely sustained the starving people. Soon their
supplies completely ran out and they were forced to search for
roots and nuts in the woods. Though they managed to survive
the winter, when Kirke returned in the summer of 1629, Quebec surrendered to the English without them having to fire a
shot. The Jesuits, including de Brébeuf, were forced to leave
the colony and return to France.

Heartbroken over leaving New France, Father Jean de
Brébeuf resolved to return someday. In the meantime, he again
took up his duties at the Jesuit College. He continued to think
about the people he yearned to minister to, and dreamed about
going back to them knowing that his dream was impossible as
long as the British continued to occupy Quebec.

But the occupation only lasted three years. Under pressure
from France, England capitulated, and in 1632, Kirke surrendered the fort. Quebec once again belonged to France, and
Cardinal Richelieu appointed Champlain lieutenant general of
New France.

During the three years of British rule, Quebec had no
priests. In 1632 two priests arrived, Paul Le Jeune, the new
Jesuit superior, Anne de Noüe (returning for the second time)

and the lay brother, Gilbert Burel. About a month later, Champlain sailed from Dieppe, along with Fathers Antoine Daniel and Ambroise Davost. In 1633, Jean de Brébeuf and Ennemond Massé also returned to New France, overjoyed to see it again after their three-year wait. No Recollet priests were sent to the colony because the French authorities did not want to support two religious orders. They believed the Jesuits could better carry out missionary work in the New World.

When the French arrived, about 700 Hurons and Algonquins came to greet Champlain and his people. The Jesuits saw their opportunity to return to Huronia. But at that time Champlain was holding an Algonquin prisoner for killing a Frenchman. Le Borgne, an Ottawa chief, urged the native people to demand the Algonquin's release, but Champlain refused this request. The Ottawa chief assembled his people and convinced them that if the Hurons agreed to transport the Jesuits, great evil would befall them. The priests would have to wait.

Meanwhile, more Hurons returned to Quebec and gradually resumed trading with the French. The native people were facing hard times, because disease had invaded their villages, and the Iroquois were at war with them. In July 1634, a party of Hurons came to trade at Three Rivers. When de Brébeuf, Daniel, and Davost learned of this, they traveled to that town to again request passage to Huronia.

At first, the Hurons shook their heads in refusal; however, they found it hard to resist the gifts of knives, kettles, and beads. They reluctantly agreed to take the three blackrobes back to Huronia, but in separate canoes. The Hurons worried that de Brébeuf would upset their canoe because of his size and all the supplies he was carting to the village. De Brébeuf knew from his past experience that he would have to kneel perfectly still in the boat. This position, on the long journey, cramped his legs, but he ignored his discomfort so as not to distress the

Hurons by upsetting the canoe. He even wore a nightcap rather than his usual large brimmed hat when the Hurons made it known that they did not like him to wear it when traveling the waters.

Davost and Daniel lacked de Brébeuf's knowledge of the Huron language, so they had a more difficult time. Davost lost his baggage, books, and personal belongings to the Ottawas. Daniel suffered a similar fate, but both men managed to continue the journey. Despite their setbacks, they pushed forward to reach the village where they could begin their missionary work.

After thirty days of travel, they landed in Huron country. Intending to reopen the mission at Toanché, de Brébeuf brought with him a large black box in which he had packed the sacred vessels and other items needed to celebrate Mass. His guides carried the box while he carried other supplies on his back and in his arms. He followed the guides who moved so quickly along the path that it was difficult for the priest to keep up. The path's constant turns right and left often caused de Brébeuf to lose sight of his escort completely. He stumbled, fell, picked up his heavy load, and continued on. Mosquitoes buzzed around his ears, biting at his face and neck; flies crawled on his cheeks and brow and he could not brush them away while carrying his load. He strained just to put one foot ahead of the other, for his feet had swollen inside his boots and hurt when he walked. Perspiration dripped from his hair and rolled down his nose, making his skin itch. The heat and humidity made the heavy black robe cling to his body like stifling armor, yet he pushed on, anxious to reach Toanché and the small chapel where he had offered Mass so many times during his first stay.

As de Brébeuf rounded a bend in the path, he saw that the guides had stopped and had gathered. One of them confronted de Brébeuf, "We are close now," and then disappeared into the thick forest. Suddenly, without explanation, the two men who had been carrying the black box set it on the ground and disappeared as well. De Brébeuf knew they were abandoning him, though he pleaded, "Remember our bargain, the promise you made." He yelled after them, "You accepted the gifts. It is wrong to leave me now." Nevertheless, they scattered in every direction and he found himself alone in the silence of the great forest. Kneeling on the path, de Brébeuf thanked God for having brought him safely this far. Then, after hiding the black box in a clump of bushes, he picked up the bundles he could carry and continued on the path. Toanché could not be far, and that thought made his aching feet move faster.

As the sun began setting in the west, casting shadows across his path, de Brébeuf trudged out of the forest into the clearing where the village of Toanché once stood. His heart sank. The chapel, the cabin, the houses—the town where he had baptized and preached for three years—were now only ashes. Charred poles indicated where the longhouses and chapel had once stood. Contemplating the ruins, de Brébeuf recalled hearing that the villagers had put Champlain's inter-preter, Etienne Brûlé, to death. Brûlé had betrayed Champlain and fled into the wilderness to live among the native people. From what he had heard, de Brébeuf surmised that Brûlé's wrongdoings among the Hurons must have been severe be-cause they had killed him and then consumed his flesh. Why the people had vacated Toanché was a mystery, but de Brébeuf knew that after a village was destroyed the Hurons usually rebuilt their settlement only a few miles from the former one. De Brébeuf knelt in the ruins and prayed for the soul of Brûlé.

The sky glowed orange behind the dark boughs of pine and de Brébeuf slowly got to his feet and followed the worn path that he instinctively knew would lead him to the Huron settle-ment. He soon came to a cluster of bark houses. The new village, which the Hurons called "Teandeouiata," looked much like the old community, except that it lacked a chapel. The idea of building a new mission was already taking shape in de Brébeuf's mind when a few villagers caught sight of his broad blackrobed figure coming out of the forest. They ran to greet him. "Echon has come back! Echon has come back!" The happy expressions on their faces made his heart sing as he hoped for more conversions, more baptisms.

When Daniel and Davost arrived days later, de Brébeuf ran to greet them. Davost looked half-starved and Daniel could barely stand up. They would lodge temporarily with Awandoay, a wealthy man who offered to share his house until the Jesuits could build a cabin. De Brébeuf made plans for the future, which looked so promising. Sitting around the hearth of the smoke-filled longhouse of Awandoay, the three priests discussed a suitable site for the mission. De Brébeuf chose a spot called Ihonatiria, not far from Teandeouiata. The people from both towns helped to construct a bark house similar to the native dwellings. The Jesuits partitioned the thirty-six foot longhouse and divided the rooms into a chapel, a kitchen or workshop, sleeping quarters, and a schoolroom. De Brébeuf painted a large cross red and mounted it on the roof of the chapel. The priests furnished the small church with an altar, a crucifix, and candles; all the precious items de Brébeuf had stored in the big black box the Hurons had recovered and brought back to him. He noticed the suspicious glances of the shaman and some of the people as they passed by the box, but de Brébeuf was too ecstatic to be back ministering among the Hurons to feel concerned.

The Jesuits named the chapel St. Joseph, and the Hurons visited the priests regularly. In time, some of the children even attended the school. The Jesuits' prism, magnet, and magnifying glass fascinated them. They regarded the clock as a marvelous thing, magical and haunting. The Hurons thought the clock was alive and they wanted to know what it ate. Just as it ended its chiming, one of the priests would raise his hand and say, "Stop!" The obedience of the clock impressed the native people, who named it "the Captain." When it struck twelve times, they knew it was time to eat, and they shared the Jesuits' sagamite (a gruel made of hominy) and whatever else the priests ate at noon. When the clock struck four times, they knew it was time to leave. The children learned the Our Father, the Hail Mary, the Creed, and other prayers, and the Jesuits rewarded their efforts with dried raisins and prunes. At the end of each day, the priests gathered around the fire and studied the Huron language. Each shared whatever he had learned about the native customs and beliefs, which made their work with the Hurons easier.

As the weather grew colder, the bone-chilling nights and hard shelves made sleeping difficult, but at least the multitude of fleas that had plagued the priests all summer had decreased somewhat. Mosquitoes also began to disappear, and only an occasional weak fly found its way into the mission house. The priests constantly attended to and prayed for the sick and the dying, sharing their meager medicines and food with the native people. They also prayed together as a community according to their rule. Although they knew that each day could be their last, they rejoiced at the thought that perhaps one day they would give their lives for the sake of the Gospel.

In 1635, a severe drought gripped the land. Without rain, the crops yielded little. Medicine men shook their rattles, chanted, danced, and sang, but the dry weather continued. The shaman at Ihonatiria danced at the entrance of St. Joseph's chapel. He said that the Jesuits had caused the trouble in the Huron land because the red cross mounted on the chapel's roof frightened away the bird of thunder. Wishing to calm the people's fears, de Brébeuf painted the cross white. Although the sound of thunder could sometimes be heard in the distance, no rain fell. The medicine men looked on the blackrobes and their practices with continued suspicion.

"Pray to God, the maker of all things," de Brébeuf encouraged. "He will help you." The people agreed to let the blackrobes try their "medicine." They held daily processions and celebrated nine Masses in honor of St. Joseph. All eyes watched the heavens for signs of rain. Clouds gathered, thunder rumbled, and the rain came to saturate the cornfields. The crops were saved!

For now, the Hurons again smiled upon the Jesuits and looked with favor upon their practices. They again respected the blackrobes and held them in high esteem. A few chiefs from neighboring villages even invited the Jesuits to come and live among them. Still, the native people did not accept Christianity.

One of their major rituals was the Feast of the Dead, which took place every ten or twelve years. Rather than burying their dead, the people placed the corpses on high scaffolds, where they remained until the Feast of the Dead. When the time for the feast arrived, the remains of the dead would be transported from nearby towns to the central location for the ceremony.

In the summer of 1636, the Feast of the Dead was held at the town of Ossossané, the home of the Bears. The chief invited de Brébeuf to participate in the feast. "Come," he said, "we will become closer...like brothers. This, the most important of our feasts, will be honored by Echon's presence." De Brébeuf agreed to attend and asked that he be allowed to bury the bones of Etienne Brûlé and the native people who had been baptized separately, in order to give them a Christian burial. It was agreed.

In this doleful ceremony, women wailed and lamented as they prepared the remains of their loved ones for burial.

According to this age-old ritual, the women wrapped the bones and corpses of their loved ones in rich furs and skins. The Hurons believed that the souls of their beloved resided in their bones. A loud lament rose on the smoke-filled evening air as de Brébeuf followed the funeral procession to the largest longhouse. Shapeless fur bundles and neat rolls of deerskins hung from the ceiling. The odor of decay that permeated the crowded dwelling made it hard for de Brébeuf to breathe. Although the people who had jammed themselves along the sides of the house crushed him against the wall, he forced himself not to retch or faint. When the longhouse ceremonies ended, all relics were taken down and brought to a common scaffold that had been erected over a large pit.

After painting their bodies and faces in blue, red, white, and black, the men led the funeral procession. Some wore tattoos from head to toe. A melancholy chant came from the women who followed, while the women and girls who were carrying sacks of food wailed the cry of the souls, "H-a-e-e! H-a-e-e! H-a-e-e!" De Brébeuf would remember this dirge for the rest of his life.

Families camped around the open pit and each group spoke in turn about the attributes of their deceased and boasted of the fine gifts they had brought for the ceremony. Attendants lined the grave with a blanket of fine furs. The master in charge of the feast would determine the time when the remains of all the dead would be placed in the communal grave. When he gave the signal, the men standing on the scaffold emptied the bags and packages while others stood in the pit arranging the bones and decaying bodies. After gifts of wampum beads, kettles, clay pipes, and bowls were also placed in the pit, layers of furs were spread to cover everything. Three very large kettles were placed on the top, one without a handle, one with a hole, and one in unusable condition. It was believed that these utensils could only be used by the spirits of the dead. Earth, stones, and logs were placed on the top of the grave, and the melancholic chanting resumed. The Hurons believed that if the bones were not buried all together and at the same time, the dead would never find peace.

Finally, the Feast of the Dead was over for another ten or twelve years. This ceremony, common to the Iroquois as well as to the Hurons, helped de Brébeuf realize how the native people's concern for the dead could provide a springboard to preach the Christian message of eternal life.

In gratitude for his participation in the feast, the chief of the Bears later presented Echon with a beaver robe. It was also in remuneration for a collar of 12,000 wampum beads that Echon had given the tribe. Echon cleverly refused the gift, saying, "You cannot thank us in any better way than by willingly listening to us tell you about the one-who-created-all and believing in him." De Brébeuf also spoke of the opportunity open to young Huron boys and men to study in the new Jesuit school at Quebec. The French hoped that this venture would cement relations between them and the Hurons, and help spread Christianity among the native people. After hearing Echon's eloquent speech, some chiefs agreed to send their sons to Quebec. The school, however, would also mean changes for the Jesuit personnel in Huronia.

The superior for all the missions in New France, Father Paul Le Jeune, recalled Daniel and Davost to Quebec to establish the school for Huron youth. Six boys traveled to Quebec, and their elders promised that more would follow if they were treated well. The Jesuits hoped this was a sign that the native people were beginning to accept the Catholic faith.

The mission in Huronia seemed lonely without Daniel and Davost. Many of the Hurons who had escaped the influenza had gone off for their seasonal hunts. Meanwhile, de

Brébeuf and the other priests, Pierre Pijart and François Joseph Le Mercier, studied the Huron language more intensely. Louis Amantacha, a Huron whom the Recollets had sent to France for a time, visited the mission and brought a bundle of letters. The priests, who had been anxiously awaiting any news, read and re-read Le Jeune's long letters. They rejoiced at the news that six more priests and two brothers had arrived at Quebec, and grieved to learn that Champlain, who had labored so hard to make Quebec and New France self-sufficient, had died.

A few days later, a runner appeared at the mission, calling out, "The blackrobe has come!" De Brébeuf found it hard to believe that a blackrobe had landed at the nearby cove, but he quickly ran down the dusty path to the water and was amazed at what he saw. Father Pierre Chastellain stepped out of a canoe and gave de Brébeuf a bear hug. Father Charles Garnier arrived the next day. Le Mercier later wrote, "The joy that is experienced in these reunions seems to be some foretaste of the happiness of the blessed upon their arrival in heaven." Gratitude and hope filled de Brébeuf's heart. One look at these men and he knew they were zealous missioners for Christ.

Chastellain and Garnier had studied together, and now they would fulfill their dream of laboring among the Hurons. Thirty-year-old Chastellain, a large man, enjoyed excellent health. Garnier was of slight build, fine-featured, and clean-shaven. The people called him "Ouracha," and Chastellain, "Airoo."

In September 1636, Father de Brébeuf received word that another priest had arrived at Ossossané. He returned there to find Isaac Jogues, a French boy named Jean Amyot, and a few workmen. The French had sent the boy as a sign of good will, since the Hurons had let some of their boys go to Quebec. Father Isaac had red hair, a beard, and delicate features. Jogues had been born into a well-to-do family and early in his life had been attracted to the Society of Jesus. Along with Chastellain and Garnier, Jogues had studied at Clermont College in Paris. De Brébeuf embraced Jogues and welcomed him to the land of the Hurons. The villagers at Ossossané later adopted him and called him "Ondessonk," a name meaning "bird of prey." Not long after Jogues arrived, he fell seriously ill.

Chapter Three

The influenza that caused such misery in the native villages had also infected the French. Its victims developed fever first, then a severe cough, followed by profuse sweating and delirium. Little Jean Amyot was struck sick, as were the workmen Mathurin and Dominique. Le Mercier, Garnier, Chastellain, and de Brébeuf, still in good health, tended the patients and prayed the epidemic would abate. Pierre Pijart and Simon Baron were away, but were expected to return soon. With the epidemic growing more serious each day, de Brébeuf worried that the priests might also fall ill.

His fears became a reality when Chastellain and Garnier caught the influenza. Jogues, meanwhile, grew steadily worse, burning with fever and coughing severely. Father de Brébeuf thought Jogues would surely die and gave him Viaticum. De Brébeuf had no medicines for the influenza, and he knew only one way to relieve fever—to bleed the patient.

With Jogues so ill, the priests agreed that he had to be bled, but who would do it? To cut him ineptly would surely kill him. De Brébeuf spoke to Jogues and asked him to name the person he trusted to act as a surgeon. Weak but alert, Jogues said he would make the cut himself. De Brébeuf brought the candle close to his arm to give him as much light as possible, then raised Jogues to a sitting position. Jogues made a clean cut in his arm, and the blood was drained off. De Brébeuf bound the wound, and Jogues lapsed into a coma.

The next day Jogues' fever had passed its crisis and, though he was very weak, he rallied. Le Mercier, who had tended his confreres without respite, was the next to come down with the fever. He asked de Brébeuf and Pijart to bleed him as they had the others, but Le Mercier did not respond to the treatment. His fever, which rose and fell, worried de Brébeuf. On the third day, Le Mercier reached a crisis point, and the priests could only pray for him. Within hours, it appeared that he would survive.

Dominique, the workman, had also fallen ill and was bled, but he did not improve. The priests soon realized that he was going to die. Shortly after Father de Brébeuf administered the last sacraments, Dominique died as the small community prayed at his bedside.

Although Pijart, de Brébeuf, and the hunter Petit-Pré remained in good health, by early October, the seven patients still had not fully recovered. The priests acknowledged God's goodness in preserving the health of three of their members, who were thus able to nurse those who had fallen ill. They considered the sickness a blessing, because the Hurons reasoned that if the priests also suffered from the influenza, then they could not be responsible for it. The epidemic began to spread among the people in early September when the traders returned from Algonquin territory. It raged through one Huron village after another. Village after village fell victim to the terrible illness, and the native people used every healing method they possessed.

Despair reigned and they turned to the shamans for help. Their leader, Tonneraouanont, interpreted dreams and commanded all who could do so to perform the ritual of dancing and singing around those who were sick. The shamans used masks to frighten away the evil spirits and chanted prayers, but the people continued to die. De Brébeuf and the other blackrobes did what they could to help the sick, providing them with nourishing broth. The Hurons understood bloodletting and even asked for it, since it appeared to have an immediate effect.

The Jesuits who were still healthy stayed at Ihonatiria, but moved from town to town, to minister to the sick, the dying, the elderly, the children, and anyone in need. All the while, they continued to preach the word of God, but without much visible result.

In the town of Wenrio, the people asked de Brébeuf to help them. "What would you have us do?" they asked. De Brébeuf answered, "Believe in God and keep his commandments. Put aside your faith in dreams; take but one wife and be true to her. Make a vow that if God will deliver you from this illness, you will build a chapel to thank and praise him." De Brébeuf studied the faces of his audience to see if they agreed, but they grumbled and shook their heads. They did not like the terms. At Ossossané, however, the people were more accepting. Terror marked every face; every family had suffered the loss of a loved one. The wailing and lamenting of children and elders rent the village. The people agreed to try whatever de Brébeuf deemed necessary.

After Jogues' recovery, he accompanied de Brébeuf and Pijart each morning and evening in their visits to the cabins to minister to the people. The priests tended to the physical needs of the native people, but they were even more concerned about their spiritual needs. The adults who were dying were baptized if they so desired, as were the children and infants in danger of death. Some would not accept Christianity, and this troubled the Jesuits.

De Brébeuf hoped that the epidemic would abate when winter came, but it only worsened as the cold winds blew and the snow began to fall. In November 1636, Fathers de Brébeuf, Jogues, and Petit-Pré traveled twelve miles to Ossossané along a path hardly visible beneath the freshly fallen snow. The biting frost nipped their hands and toes. On their arrival, the people of Ossossané welcomed the blackrobes; they liked Echon and wanted to see Jogues, now known as Ondessonk. Nevertheless, they disregarded the words of the Jesuits. Some believed that the blackrobes had caused the disease and said that the Hurons died because of the pouring on of water at baptism, or the broth that the blackrobes brought to the sick. When the priests returned to Ihonatiria, they heard the same rumors. Although their work grew more difficult, they continued their ministry, not knowing what winter would bring.

By February, the snow was piled high against the longhouses and silently creeped under the skins that hung over the doorways. The people sat around the fires in the smoke-filled longhouses and dreamed of the spring. In the spring, the men would mend their nets, board canoes, and travel down the river to fish and hunt beaver. They would once again walk the leafy woodland paths and search for game. The women would once again till the damp, dark earth to plant their corn and squash while they laughed and talked. The influenza victims grew less, and the people's spirits improved.

In late February 1637, a chief named Tsiouendaentaha approached Echon and requested baptism, saying that he had learned much about God from the Jesuits. De Brébeuf wondered at the request. It seemed strange that this chief, one who had great influence at the council fires, would ask for baptism just when some of the people were accusing the Jesuits of sorcery. He might prove, however, to be the answer to Echon's prayers. If Tsiouendaentaha was sincere and became a faithful Christian, this might lay the groundwork for future conversions.

Garnier and de Brébeuf instructed Tsiouendaentaha, who proved intelligent and enthusiastic in his promise to live a Christian life. In June, the chief invited all the men of Ihonatiria to attend a great feast during which his baptism would take place; he wanted everyone to witness the ceremony. The priests decorated their longhouse with wildflowers and green branches. They constructed an altar at one end of the room, placed lighted candles nearby, and displayed their sacred pictures and statues. The people crowded in, straining to see Father de Brébeuf pour the water on Tsiouendaentaha's head. The chief clearly spoke his renunciations of sin and Satan, and made his promises solemnly for all to hear. De Brébeuf poured the water, baptizing the chief in the name of the Father, the Son, and the Holy Spirit. He was given the Christian name "Peter." Echon celebrated Mass, and Peter received his first Holy Communion.

In Peter's honor, Echon invited everyone to the special feast. The delicious aroma of cornmeal and boiled fish wafted on the breeze, and one by one the people came. The beauty of the decorations impressed them, and the sacred images sparked their curiosity. Were the statues alive? Could the pictures talk? When the guests saw a painting of the Last Judgment, fear filled their hearts. A hushed stillness fell over the room as the people lingered to examine the painting.

De Brébeuf's zeal increased. Peter was a beginning; more conversions would surely follow. The priests had learned the

Huron language well, and more Jesuits would arrive in September. De Brébeuf originated a plan that would enable the Jesuits to serve more of the Huron people. They would continue the mission at Ihonatiria and establish new missions in larger villages as well, moving farther and farther out. De Brébeuf believed that the priests should live among the people in the villages in order to learn more about their customs and beliefs. Ossossané seemed to be the best location for the central mission. De Brébeuf proceeded wisely and cautiously, asking the privilege to speak at the council meeting.

The chiefs listened as de Brébeuf told them of his hopes and plans. They liked Echon and agreed to build him a longhouse outside the palisades, yet close to the village as he requested. De Brébeuf thought that the location outside the village would allow more privacy for the priests. The construction of the house, sixty feet long and eighteen feet wide, began almost immediately. The priests placed the new mission under the protection of Mary, the Immaculate Conception.

For now the epidemic seemed to have spent itself, but de Brébeuf feared that once the warm weather returned, the influenza might come back. Former suspicions surfaced anew at Teanaustayé. Now it was whispered that the blackrobes' sugar, which the Hurons called "French Snow," was poison. The rumors abounded, and some even suggested that the blackrobes had caused the disease that killed so many. They claimed that the Jesuits kept a dead body to serve them in their black magic, and that something in the small box on the altar was causing their death.

De Brébeuf's fears were realized in July of 1637 when illness struck once again. It only served to convince the people that the blackrobes caused the disease. Many urged the chiefs to drive the priests out of the village. Toward the end of July, de Brébeuf visited the Rock Nation, where he heard the chiefs at

Angwiens believed that killing a Frenchman would halt the illness. De Brébeuf thought he could convince the chiefs that killing a Frenchman would not quell the disease. He wrote to Le Mercier, warning him to avoid Angwiens. In the meantime, a rumor spread that de Brébeuf had been murdered. When he finally returned to Ossossané, Le Mercier greeted his confrere as if he had risen from the dead. Everyone, including the Jesuits, believed that Echon had been killed.

In August 1637, the Hurons held a great council to investigate the cause of the terrible sickness that ravaged the villages, and invited de Brébeuf and Le Mercier. They convened also to consider war or peace with the Seneca Iroquois, who were becoming more hostile. As the chiefs debated the cause of the epidemic, one of them, aged and ailing, pointed a finger at Echon. He appraised the priest through narrowed eyes and nodded. He declared that the blackrobes knew something about the cause of the influenza, and perhaps were its cause. De Brébeuf and Le Mercier sat beside warriors who carried weapons, and they knew that their lives were in danger. The attendants of the council grew sullen and de Brébeuf did not see many friendly faces among them. He replied to the accusations by denying the charges. As always, he spoke eloquently and the chiefs listened closely to his words. The younger chiefs accused the blackrobes of hiding in their cabin a cloth that was inhabited by a demon. This demon, they said, was causing the Huron to die. De Brébeuf denied having any knowledge of the cause of the sickness, and reminded them that members in his own community had been stricken. This did not quell the old suspicions, and the meeting ended without resolution.

Although the elder chiefs had temporarily restrained the younger men, the threat of death still hung over the Jesuit's longhouse. The warriors boasted that they had already split the skulls of two witches and would soon kill the blackrobes. The older chiefs tried to stall. They persuaded the younger ones to wait until the traders returned from Three Rivers and Quebec. De Brébeuf hoped that Governor de Montmagny would calm the people's fears and the agitation.

Father de Brébeuf and the other priests prayed even more intensely that the epidemic might end. They celebrated Masses in honor of St. Joseph and the Blessed Virgin, but more people became infected every day. One morning another victim of the influenza, the Huron chief, Chihwatenhwa, dragged himself to Echon's longhouse. While the Jesuits nursed him, Chihwatenhwa's told de Brébeuf that he had only one wife and that he no longer believed in the use of charms. Chihwatenhwa declared that he believed all that Echon preached and begged to be baptized. The priests at Ossossané offered a novena in honor of St. Joseph that the chief might live. When Chihwatenhwa finally recovered, he promised to live as a faithful Christian. De Brébeuf, assuring himself that the chief was sincere, baptized him and gave him the name Joseph. Joseph gave a feast for his friends and relatives, and, to the astonishment of the Hurons, spoke of the glory of God. Some months later, his wife Aonetta was also baptized. Joseph would prove a most faithful Christian.

Around this time Father de Brébeuf experienced a vision, and wrote about it as follows:

On the twenty-first, it might be the twenty-second or the twenty-third, of August, during the evening examination of conscience and the litany of the Blessed Virgin, by an actual or an imaginary vision, I seemed to see a vast throng of demons coming toward me to devour me or, at least, to bite me. But not one could harm me.... That apparition lasted perhaps for the space of a *Miserere*. I do not recall that I was frightened, but I placed my confidence in God, saying: "Do to me whatever God allows you to do. You will not pluck out a hair of my head without his assent and command." ... At other times I saw death with hands bound to a post near me, endeavoring to spring forward in a fury, but unable to break the bonds with which it was restrained, until it fell at my feet without strength or vigor, powerless to hurt me.

To live with the knowledge that death could come at any moment: at prayer in the longhouse, in the cabins of the sick, or on the paths in the forests—at any place and at any time—must have given de Brébeuf and the other missionaries an awareness unknown to most people. They lived in virtual isolation, without any means of defense or protection, trusting in God, knowing that only he could decide when death would come. All they could do was to remain ready.

While the Huron confederacy was holding their council meetings, word came that the Iroquois were forcing the Wenrôhronons out of their country. The Wenrôhronons lived in the land west of the Neutrals and were distant relatives of the Bear Nation, who decided to give them asylum. They offered their land and their homes to about 600 refugees, many of them women and children. A large party of warriors traveled 200 miles to escort the Wenrôhronons to Ossossané and, by mid-August, they arrived: chiefs, men, women, and children. The people of Ossossané greeted them warmly, opening their stores of corn to them and providing them with homes. The Bears decreed that the Wenrôhronons and the Hurons would become one people.

De Brébeuf and the other Jesuits also welcomed the Wenrôhronons cordially, offering them food and what little medicines they had. Many of the strangers were either ill from the long journey or suffering from the epidemic. The priests administered baptism to as many of the dying as accepted it and they tended to the needs of the living. The population of Ossossané literally grew overnight.

Occasionally a cry would erupt during the day, a warning that the Iroquois were approaching the vicinity. "Ho-de-no-sau-nee! Ho-de-no-sau-nee! The Iroquois! The Iroquois!" When they heard these warnings, the women would gather their children and any food they could take and ran to the woods and thickets to hide. Men would scramble to secure their tomahawks and bows and arrows that were always close by. And the Jesuits would wait for the Iroquois, praying for the safety of the Hurons. But the Iroquois did not come. The people went back to their homes, apprehensive and uneasy.

CHAPTER FOUR

Although the Iroquois threat continued to hang over Huronia, the Jesuits continued their missionary work. More priests traveled from Quebec: Father Antoine Daniel returned to Ossossané in July 1638, and in August, Father Jerome Lalemant arrived by canoe. Fathers Simon Le Moyne and François Du Peron followed in September. Lalemant brought with him a letter that appointed him as superior to replace de Brébeuf. De Brébeuf gladly relinquished his authority because he believed that the position of leadership should have been given to someone holier and more worthy than himself. All the other Jesuits disagreed with him. De Brébeuf was their guiding light in the darkness of the forests, a saint among the Hurons, a wise and compassionate confrere whom they deeply respected. Although they welcomed the change in a spirit of obedience, they did were not so sure of the Hurons' reaction. The people regarded de Brébeuf as a great chief. Would they accept that another French chief had come to take his place as leader? De Brébeuf had been the first to study the Huron language and he spoke it fluently. The chiefs listened to him and admired his courage, strength, and intelligence. They had come to respect Echon.

Like de Brébeuf, Lalemant was forty-five years old. He had an impeccable scholastic record, was a noted professor of philosophy, and possessed administrative skills. The new superior immediately assigned new duties, sending de Brébeuf, Isaac Jogues, and two younger men, Paul Ragueneau and Simon Le Moyne, to Teanaustayé. Lalemant remained at Ossossané with François Le Mercier, Pierre Chastellain, Charles Garnier, and François Du Peron. He established a new schedule as well. At five o'clock in summer and four in winter, the doors of the mission would now be closed to all Hurons. The priests were to retire at nine every evening. The Jesuit community did not complain about the end of their informal style of living; however, the Hurons did not like the changes. The blackrobes had always left their doors open to them and they were free to enter at any time. There had always been time to listen to the priests praying or complaining. There had always been a pot of sagamite cooking on the hearth fire and it was generously offered to anyone who wished to partake of it.

Jerome Lalemant was unbending regarding his policies. "Our initial step," he said, "will be to travel all over the country which was the first to receive us, and take a census. Then we shall push farther on, always farther on, until we have accomplished our task, which is only bounded by the setting sun."

One of Lalemant's innovations was the formation of a group of laymen who were called *donnés*. They differed from the helpers, or *engagés*, who were workmen of good character. The *engagés* were men who assisted the Jesuits in their work, and they were also allowed to participate in the fur trade. The *donnés* were men who felt drawn to the Society of Jesus, but did not wish to make religious vows. They observed a life of chastity and they were bound to obedience to the priests, and helped the missionaries in their work. These men were obliged by a civil contract and received no wages, but were clothed, fed and cared for if sick.

Because Lalemant wanted to gather all available information about the country and the native people, he detained Jean de Brébeuf at Ossossané. They discussed the affairs of the natives, the state of the missions, and their future there. Lalemant relied upon de Brébeuf's knowledge and skill, and questioned him about the population and location of the Huron villages. De Brébeuf shared everything he had learned in working with the Hurons. Lalemant wanted to establish a permanent central mission where all the priests would reside, and they would travel to appointed areas. This conflicted with de Brébeuf's desire to establish many missions that could make the priests available to the people at all times. However, de Brébeuf cooperated in every way possible with Lalemant's plans, though they differed from his own ideas.

When the discussions finally ended, de Brébeuf left Ossossané quickly, anxious to return to his ministry among the Hurons. But accusations began surfacing again because a few villagers had fallen ill. The people blamed the blackrobes for bringing disease to destroy the Huron Nation. It broke de Brébeuf's heart to see the children he had once taught catechism hurling stones and sticks at him and the other priests as they walked through the village. The adults behaved similarly, but the Jesuits bore this ordeal with compassion and charity.

Despite the difficulties, their work was bearing fruit. Jogues and de Brébeuf baptized an elderly chief who renounced his former ways to serve God: Aochiati declared his faith publicly and was baptized and given the name "Matthias." Two of his young granddaughters received baptism with him on December 20, 1638. The priests baptized eleven other people two days later. On the first day of the New Year, about fifteen people attended Mass.

Heartened by this success, Lalemant pursued his goal and began building the central mission. It would not only serve as a residence for the priests, but as a hospital, fort, school, and convent. He made plans to plant gardens and bring in pigs and cows from Quebec, so that the mission could provide for all its needs. The site for this central mission, called Sainte Marie, was on the banks of the River Wye. Here the priests had access to all parts of the Huron territory. The missions at Ossossané and Teanaustayé were eventually abandoned, but not before the Jesuits had visited every Huron town and given each a saint's name. Now they would move out into the land of the Petuns, or Tobacco Nation, nine towns located south of Ihonatiria. The priests had divided the Huron towns into four districts, and the Tobacco Nation would make the fifth. Lalemant assigned Jogues and Garnier to begin the mission to the Petuns.

The journey to their country was dangerous in good weather and far more perilous in the winter. Yet, in November 1639 as the first snow fell, the two priests set out on foot. Falling thick and fast, the snow obscured the path that led away from Ossossané. Jogues and Garnier belted up their robes, donned leggings, boots, fur mittens, and woolen caps over which they placed their large-brimmed hats. They adjusted their backpacks, heavy with the trinkets, knives, and beads they were bringing as presents for the Petuns. At their waists hung the snowshoes they would need later. They had left Ossossané in early morning with a meager supply of food, staffs in hand, their bodies bent from the weight of their packs. They hoped to reach the town of Ehwae before night, but the falling snow and cold wind slowed them down. As they passed through the boggy lowland, water seeped into their boots, and icicles formed on their eyebrows and beards. It was dark when Jogues motioned to Garnier, directing him to a grove of trees. Fir tree branches interlaced overhead and, with the cold wind swirling all around them, they looked for firewood, but only found wet branches. They ate their dry bread, spread their blankets, and wrapped themselves for the night, praying that tomorrow the Petuns would welcome the Lord's word. Later they wrote, "God be blessed, we spent the night very comfortably."

When morning's light pierced through the forest, they started out again in the deep snow toward the village of Ehwae. Over a rise, the missionaries caught sight of a few scattered houses, but the people seemed to move about dispiritedly, heads bowed and backs bent. Their crops had failed and their storehouses of corn and food were now empty. They were preparing to abandon their dwellings and travel to Ehwae. Jogues and Garnier decided to join the band of migrants, and at nightfall, they came to the first village of the Petuns, which the priests named St. Thomas.

Having eaten nothing all day, they gratefully accepted the bowls of sagamite that the people offered them. While they were resting on a mat by the fire, a young man burst into the cabin. He pleaded with the priests to attend to his mother, who was at the point of death. After briefly instructing her, they baptized the woman, who then died peacefully.

From St. Thomas they followed the trails that led deeper into Petun country and, as the little band passed through many small villages along the way, the priests baptized a few children and some adults who were dying. The Petuns welcomed the Jesuits because the Hurons had adopted Ondessonk and Ouracha, making them brothers to the Petuns as well. None of the villagers had ever seen a white man, and the novelty of the Jesuits' appearance bewildered them. They touched the faces of their adopted brothers, studied their clothing, and inspected their baggage.

The priests finally reached Ehwae in mid-November and dedicated the village to Saints Peter and Paul. Out of courtesy to the chief of Ehwae, Ondessonk and Ouracha went directly to his dwelling. Although he offered his hospitality, he did not accept their gifts, nor did he listen to any proposals. He was too absorbed in other matters: the Attiwandaron, or Neutral Nation, was migrating en masse to Petun villages. The Neutrals' crops had failed, and they now faced starvation.

The missionaries reported, "There is hardly any corn in the village of Ehwae. Nevertheless, almost every day some Attiwandarons arrive, bands of men, women, and children, all pale and disfigured, whom the famine drives here. Fleeing from the famine, here they find death; rather, here they find a blessed life, for we see to it that not one dies without baptism."

The Petuns understood the Huron dialect, and the priests spoke to them of God, of his great goodness, and of life everlasting for those who accepted his word. Though the Petuns listened, they did not welcome the preaching of the Jesuits, but stood there with stern faces and an unreadable expression in their eyes.

The supply of corn at Ehwae dwindled to almost nothing. The threat of starvation became a stark reality. Malnourished and ill, the people grew agitated and short-tempered. Therefore, when a band of Huron traders came through Ehwae and accused the blackrobes of causing all the people's troubles, the Petuns' no longer extended their hospitality. Mothers hid their children when the priests approached; people no longer allowed them into their houses. Jogues and Garnier decided that nothing could be gained at Ehwae, so they went in search of other villages.

December winds were blowing colder now, and the falling snow piled high in drifts. The priests braced themselves against a winter storm, and left the Petun village with halting steps and heavy hearts.

They came to a cluster of small houses huddled against the foot of a hill, only to find that Petun runners had preceded them with bad reports about the blackrobes. Village after village was closed to Ondessonk and Ouracha. Some chiefs threatened to kill them if they came closer, and the priests were forced to turn back into the forests. They had no shelter, no place to sleep, nothing to eat; they were outcasts. Some nights they slept in the hollows of snow they dug.

One morning, weak and near starving, Jogues and Garnier trudged into a small village. Crude dwellings were nestled together under a blanket of snow. In their desperation, the priests had no choice but to force themselves into a cabin. Jogues was feverish, and both he and Garnier needed nourishment. However grudgingly, the people did give them minimal hospitality, so the priests decided to rest there before moving on. But a runner came from one of the Petun villages Jogues and Garnier had visited. He brought news that the people were asking for Ondessonk and Ouracha to return to their village, thirty-five miles away. Despite Jogues' weakness, hearing God's call in the request from the Petuns, he and Garnier put on their snowshoes and set out for the Petun village long before dawn. The bitterly cold air made breathing painful; each step through the ice-crusted snow was an effort. They did not dare to stop for long for fear they would die of the cold.

They arrived at the village chilled to the bone, but safe and they praised God. Some of the people were still alive. In a smoke-filled cabin, people lay on their mats covered with smallpox. The groans of the dying and the cries of suffering infants tore at the hearts of the Jesuits. They thanked God that they had come in time to administer baptism. The priests were able to rest a little at this village, and during their stay Joseph Chihwatenhwa, the Christian of Ossossané, visited them. Later they wrote that he came "in the midst of weather that was frightful, while the cold was cracking the trees and a furious wind was blowing in his face. The fire of his charity was greater than all these inclemencies." Joseph had heard that

Ouracha and Ondessonk's lives were in danger, and he believed that he could persuade the Petuns to receive the Jesuits in a kindly manner. He had already helped Daniel and Le Moyne, whom the Arendarhonon Hurons had maltreated.

Joseph brought news of Ossossané. The smallpox had entered every cabin, but God had spared him. His wife, Aonetta, fearing the disease and for her sons and daughter Theresa, had begged Joseph not to leave. Nevertheless, he left with the faith that God would protect his family from the illness and that he would return to them safely. Joseph's unexpected appearance not only surprised the priests, but also encouraged and strengthened them. They thanked God for this blessing. They left the cabin and traveled to another village a day's journey away, arriving just as the sun was sinking behind the dark forest. When they pulled back the skin from the door of a longhouse, the people turned them away with angry words. They went to another cabin but received the same treatment. Joseph's relatives in the village could not refuse hospitality to him and to the blackrobes, but they made Ondessonk and Ouracha promise to leave in the morning.

The next day they reached a village on the outskirts of Ehwae whose people had once received the blackrobes warmly, but now no one would allow them to enter their longhouse. One old man, who had listened to the Jesuits' words with interest in the past, called out, "You are welcome" and offered a place by the fire. Despite Joseph's influence, the other villagers shunned the blackrobes. The Petuns believed the Jesuits were working evil spells against them to destroy them. The people of Ehwae not only closed their homes to the priests, but they threatened to split the blackrobes' heads if they ever showed themselves again. The reappearance of Ouracha and Ondessonk fanned the flames of fear and anger. The chiefs held council and declared the blackrobes sorcerers and enemies of the people who worked secretly to destroy the Petuns, the Hurons, and all the tribes. Weapons in hand, a group of young men traveled swiftly in pursuit the priests and Joseph who had taken shelter with a family in a small village. As long as they were under the householder's protection, the young men could not enter. They returned home frustrated and furious.

The following day a group of men led by the chief of Ehwae came to apologize for the "rash actions" of the young warriors. Joseph recognized their insincerity and he tried to explain that the blackrobes were bringing a message of grave importance to the people. The chief said he did not believe anyone could take the blackrobes seriously. Annoyed by his response, Joseph countered, "You drive away those who love you more than themselves; they count their own lives less precious than your salvation. They come here from a great distance and with very many labors to obtain your salvation."

The chief listened politely and some people even nodded agreement, but Joseph's speech did not sway them. With no other alternatives left to them, the priests and Joseph had to leave the Petun country. Jogues and Garnier had tried their best to preach the message of God's love to the Petuns and they vowed to return.

The priests' stay in the land of the Petuns was not entirely fruitless. They had taken the opportunity to sketch maps of the country with its trails, distances, and exact directions. They had named nine major towns after the apostles, and estimated the population to be about 1,000 families. They had baptized many and had spoken of God to thousands more. They would return at a more favorable time, trying again to bring the word of God to the Petun Nation.

Lalemant wrote to France, "This mission to the Petuns has been the richest of all, since there the crosses and the sufferings have been the most abundant."

CHAPTER FIVE

While Jogues and Garnier were spending the winter of 1639–1640 in the country of the Petuns, Lalemant remained at Sainte Marie with Pijart and Poncet. Ragueneau took charge of Ossossané; Daniel and Le Moyne were assigned to the eastern and southern part of Huronia to open a new mission among the Arendarhonons, the Rock Nation. De Brébeuf and Pierre Joseph Chaumonot, a priest who had recently come from France, went to Teanaustayé.

Smallpox spread everywhere again. At Teanaustayé it crept into the dark longhouses, silenced the voices of children at play, and brought sickness and death to most. De Brébeuf knew that many would fall sick and that the people would think the blackrobes had been the cause. Above all, he feared that the new Christians would weaken in their baptismal commitment, and perhaps even stop him from baptizing those who were suffering from smallpox or influenza.

De Brébeuf and Chaumonot continued to visit the sick at Teanaustayé, washing their sores and giving nourishment, knowing that they risked contracting the diseases. But they rejoiced at the opportunity to baptize the dying. The priests advised the people to use separate utensils and mats for the sick, but the people still did not trust them. Children hid from the blackrobes; mothers cried out in fear whenever the priests approached. The men cursed them as they went about their business, but the priests continued to pray and teach the Christian message.

Meanwhile, a new rumor was quickly spreading through the villages: The French *engagé* Le Coq, who had survived an earlier bout with smallpox, had suddenly died. According to the rumor, before he died Le Coq swore that the blackrobes were responsible for the diseases which had come to the Huron tribes, and that the blackrobes had given him smallpox. He supposedly also said that the priests had an ancient serpent that brought disease hidden in their quarters, and that they kept a pockmarked toad that was really a demon. Before his last breath, Le Coq was supposed to have pleaded with the Hurons to kill the blackrobes.

Hurons returning from Sainte Marie brought the news that Le Coq was actually alive; they had seen him there. His sores had healed, he was well, and he denied that he had made any so-called deathbed "confession." The chiefs now began to believe that the blackrobes could not only strike people with disease, but they could also cure them, and regarded Echon as the greatest demon of all. They held councils at Teanaustayé, and de Brébeuf was once again asked to respond to their charges. He explained to a group of old men that the blackrobes had not come to the Hurons for furs and wealth, but for the sole purpose of teaching truths that would assure the people of life everlasting. Though puzzled by the events they attributed to the coming of the priests, the old men showed interest in their preaching and asked to learn more.

By November 1639, de Brébeuf and Chaumonot had assembled a group of about thirty Hurons who seemed to be sincere in their desire to become Christians. However, when de Brébeuf spoke of heaven, the people doubted such beautiful promises. Would they have tobacco in heaven? What would they eat? Could they hunt and get married? De Brébeuf continued his efforts to teach them about Christ despite setbacks. Aochiati, the chief who had embraced Christianity, now renounced it, along with some others who had received baptism at the same time. Although deeply disappointed by this, de Brébeuf did not lose hope. Ihonatiria had its Peter and Ossossané had its Joseph. Certainly others would come, other examples to shine like stars among the Hurons.

Hostilities continued and the priests feared for their lives now more than ever. In April 1640 de Brébeuf wrote:

On the eleventh of April, a quarrel arose at St. Joseph's residence. Pierre Boucher was wounded in the arm and Father Chaumonot and I were beaten. We were all suffering from injuries and were much afraid because we had been ordered to leave the village by Ondihorrea and other leaders of that village. Later I was giving thanks to God for all these things. Though disturbed in mind and being in distress, I was striving nonetheless to conform my will to the divine. And I seemed to see the Blessed Virgin, in the manner that she is depicted in sorrow, with three swords in her wounded heart. I felt interiorly as if she were telling me that, although she was sorely afflicted, she, the Blessed Mother of God, was nevertheless always conformed to the divine will and ought to be an example to me in all my adversity.

One warm afternoon as the Jesuits worked outside on some repairs to the cabin, de Brébeuf suddenly stared up at the sky and stretched out his arms. Father Chaumonot and the workmen put aside their tools and asked, "What is it?" as they looked up at the cloudless sky.

De Brébeuf's eyes were fixed toward the south in the direction of the Ho-de-no-sau-nee, the land of the Iroquois. He sighed and shook his head, saying, "It is a cross." No one else saw it. "How large is it?" they asked. De Brébeuf paused and, in a barely audible voice, answered, "It is large enough to crucify us all."

August 1640 marked a moment of great sorrow for all the priests. They heard that Joseph Chihwatenhwa, searching in the forest for cedar to build a canoe, had been killed by two strokes of a tomahawk. After the chiefs investigated, they concluded that he had been killed by an Iroquois. Joseph's death shocked the Jesuits; they had hoped that Joseph would help in converting the Hurons, and they had relied on him as an invaluable assistant. Lalemant expressed the impact Joseph's death had upon the community, stating that it could conceivably be "put in the number of the profound secrets and of the adorable dispensations of Divine Providence, a thing we cannot think upon without astonishment. Since the saints have more power when they are in heaven than here below on earth, we are bound to believe that we have gained more than we lost at his death."

They soon experienced some of those gains, which the Jesuits attributed to Joseph's intercession from heaven. To the astonishment of the Jesuits Joseph's brother, Teondechoren, asked to be baptized. Teondechoren had always opposed their teaching and had lived an immoral life. At first, de Brébeuf was not convinced of his sincerity and made him wait in order to determine his resolve to live a Christian life. Teondechoren held fast to his desire and proved his sincerity to the satisfaction of de Brébeuf who baptized him. The new convert became a faithful Christian, one who helped to bring others to the faith.

The general hostility toward the Jesuits soon began to diminish. At Sainte Marie the workmen cleared trees in order to plant corn and other crops. They gathered large stones for additional building and waited for tools and other equipment to arrive from Quebec. In September, Father Claude Pijart (the brother of Father Pierre), and Father Charles Raymbault arrived by canoe, but had been unable to bring any supply canoes with them. Notre Dame de Recouvrance in Quebec, the building where the Jesuits stored their supplies for the Huron country, had burned down.

While the native people held their councils around their fires, the Jesuits held their own meetings to appraise the results of their efforts. Though the priests had preached the Christian message to thousands of Hurons and Petuns, no more than fifty had converted to the faith. The priests estimated that the Huron population was about 12,000, while four years earlier de Brébeuf had tallied it at about 30,000. It disturbed the Jesuits to see how the epidemics and wars had taken their toll.

In their zealous efforts to preach the Gospel, the missionaries realized that, because of the decreasing Huron population, they would have to expand their outreach. Garnier and Pierre Pijart returned to the Petuns. Jogues and Du Peron were assigned to minister to the Ataronchronons, whose villages were located near Sainte Marie. Chastellain, Raymbault, and Claude Pijart also remained at Sainte Marie and ministered to the Algonquins who were camped nearby. Lalemant and Le Mercier resided at Ossossané, while Daniel and Le Moyne were assigned areas from Teanaustayé down to Cahiagué. De Brébeuf and Chaumonot traveled deep into the land of the Neutrals to carve out a new territory, one that bordered on the land of the Iroquois.

Winter again brought its bitter cold and snow, freezing the rivers and streams, glazing the forest trails with sheets of ice. In March 1641, de Brébeuf fell on the ice and broke his collarbone. The pain slowed him down, but he never complained. However, by May, the injury had still not healed and Lalemant sent de Brébeuf back to Quebec to recuperate. There he could take time to rest from his seven long years among the Hurons. As the party began the long journey, de Brébeuf prayed that, with his physical strength renewed, he would return once again to devote his spiritual talents and love of God in his ministry to the Hurons.

They arrived safely in Three Rivers at the end of June, having avoided any contact with Iroquois war parties. De Brébeuf met with Father Barthélemy Vimont, who was the Jesuit superior of New France. Father Vimont assigned de Brébeuf to work at the mission in Sillery, a few miles from Quebec. Among other tasks, he procured supplies for the Huron mission and worked in the school the Jesuits had established for young men from the native tribes. De Brébeuf stayed in Sillery until 1644.

While there, he heard reports that Iroquois raids were becoming more frequent. Beginning in 1641, the Iroquois had launched serious efforts to gain control of the fur trade. The resources in the Iroquois country had dried up, and the five Iroquois Nations—the Oneida, Onondaga, Cayuga, Seneca, and Mohawk—had to find new fur supplies in order to continue trading with the Dutch. This brought them into conflict with the Algonquins and Hurons, who controlled access to the fur trade routes in the west. The animosity between the tribes predated Champlain, and the hostility had come to involve the French in the early days of New France. The Iroquois' increased need for trade routes brought the situation to a crucial point in the early 1640s.

The Iroquois had always fought with their traditional weapons, but the Dutch at Albany were now supplying them with muskets. The Mohawks, considered the most aggressive tribe, made their home near Albany. Of their 800 warriors, 300 had muskets, which they used expertly.

Clanships bound the nations, whose government was a form of oligarchy, yet was somewhat democratic. Chiefs held office by heredity right and by election, and the women had much influence in the selection of chiefs. The Iroquois had a reputation as the most feared of the native tribes. While the Senecas concentrated on eliminating the Hurons and Algonquins, the Mohawks set their sights on destroying the French.

The entire population of Quebec trembled at the possibility of Iroquois attack. Montreal, the infant French settlement located near Quebec, was the most vulnerable. The French colonists in New France did what they could to protect themselves, and pleaded with the French government to send soldiers to defend them.

The Hurons, too, prepared to meet the threat. In the spring, when the sun warmed and renewed the earth, the Huron women planted the seeds for the fall harvest. They no longer sang or laughed as they worked, but paused to look over their shoulders, anticipating the war whoop of the Ho-de-no-sau-nee. War chiefs streaked their bodies and faces with red paint and walked through the villages carrying war poles. The Huron leaders drove the poles into the ground and the warriors attacked them with a ferocity that symbolized the death of the Iroquois. Emotions were heightened by war songs and speeches, and the Huron warriors set out into the forest to search for their enemies.

Determined to fight to the death to save their nation, many Hurons returned from their search only to report that they found no trace of the Iroquois. Other war parties had been killed or captured. With Dutch muskets and powder, the Iroquois had the advantage. Word had spread that the Iroquois had penetrated the land of the Nipissings and controlled the waterways to Quebec. Yet, the Hurons were undaunted; if they were to trade with the French, they would have to transport furs and skins through the blockade.

In June 1642, at Sainte Marie, Father Lalemant needed to send one of the priests to Quebec to deliver letters, make reports, and purchase supplies for the winter. He pondered the situation with sadness, knowing that whomever he chose would be in constant danger. He had to choose someone with experience, so Lalemant presented his dilemma to Jogues, neither asking nor commanding him, but Jogues understood the situation and willingly offered to go.

Jogues knew the dangers well and the chances of reaching his destination safely. He later confessed that as soon as he learned of the mission to Quebec, he believed God was preparing him for some extraordinary trial:

Obedience laid before me a simple proposition, not a command, to go down to Quebec, in such a way that I would not have to accept it if I were unwilling. I did not say a word against it, nor did I try to escape from it. Gladly and willingly did I accept this charge put before me by obedience and charity. I offered myself with all my heart and that the more willingly, because the necessity of undertaking this journey might have cast another of the priests, much more valuable than I, into the perils and hazards of which we were all aware.

Father Charles Raymbault would accompany Jogues. The frail priest had grown weaker with each passing season, and the community suspected that he had contracted tuberculosis. They hoped he would be able to recover in the hospital at Quebec. Guillaume Coûture, a *donné*, was asked to accompany the party and he agreed. Two Frenchmen and a number of Christian Hurons, experts in handling boats, would also travel with them.

The evening before departing for Quebec, the two priests prayed in the quiet chapel as the shadows lengthened and the candles burned brightly, a symbol of hope. Morning would come soon, and with it, the long journey ahead.

At dawn on a balmy June morning, the Christians of the village gathered in prayer with the small party about to depart as Father Lalemant blessed each one. They climbed aboard the waiting canoes and soon the rough river carried them swiftly along. The trip went quite well as they traveled the route to the Ojibwas. When they entered the Ottawa River, however, the angry waters tossed them about and almost threw them over a waterfall. Without the strong Hurons, who expertly handled the canoes, they would all have perished. They had to navigate many dangerous portages and lost some furs and supplies.

The five Frenchmen and the Hurons who accompanied them were keenly aware that the Iroquois could be waiting anywhere along the shores. The trees, the reeds, and the rushes might all be concealing the enemy. Raymbault suffered from dampness and exposure, but after thirty-five harrowing days, the small band finally arrived at Three Rivers, and then moved on to Quebec.

A burly figure hurried to the shore to meet the canoes as they landed. Father de Brébeuf embraced Jogues with his one good arm as the other still hung in a sling. After the happy exchange of greetings, de Brébeuf led everyone to the Jesuit's house where Jogues and Raymbault were served a hot meal and made to rest. There would be time later for discussion.

In the evening, de Brébeuf wanted to know everything that had happened at the missions during his absence. Jogues also asked for news of Quebec, and learned that the Duchesse d'Aiguillon, a niece of Cardinal Richelieu, and Madame de la Peltrie, a pious and wealthy widow, had come to New France along with Mother Marie de l'Incarnation and other Ursuline and Augustinian nuns. They had founded the Hôtel Dieu, a school for young women, and an Ursuline convent in Quebec.

The Jesuit College and seminary for the instruction of young converts had also been opened. Jeanne Mance, a beautiful and pious young woman who was inspired by the *Relations*, pledged financial support to the Hôtel Dieu. The *Relations'* recounting of the trials, tribulations, and successes of the Canadian missions, had generated a remarkable degree of attention from the wealthy religious population. Mance also played a significant role in founding the new settlement of Ville Marie (or Montreal, as it would later be called) in 1642. The colony of Quebec, however, had not grown much; New France still had less than 400 colonists and only 300 soldiers to guard the settlements.

Jogues heard that Father Paul le Jeune had returned to France to try to rouse concern and win financial backing for the Jesuit missions in the New World. Le Jeune also hoped to persuade Cardinal Richelieu to take action to curb the Iroquois threat and perhaps even eject the Dutch from their settlements along the Hudson River. The Iroquois impeded the Huron fur trade and drove the Algonquins away from their settlements near Quebec. Unless something was done, the colonists would not be able to remain in New France.

Cardinal Richelieu appropriated a sizable sum of money to build fortifications. The first of these, Fort Richelieu, was strategically located between Montreal and Three Rivers at the mouth of the St. Lawrence River. From here, patrols could scout for Iroquois war parties. Money was also made available for a fort at Sainte Marie among the Hurons. Soldiers there would garrison the forts and escort the Huron traders on their journeys to Three Rivers, Montreal, and Quebec.

After sharing all their news, Jogues relaxed by a large stone fireplace with Vimont and de Brébeuf. Vimont was eager to hear Jogues' report about the victories for Christ at Sainte Marie. Jogues carefully related everything he could to his superior. The mission was succeeding, but the Iroquois posed a great threat. Jogues asked, even begged, to be sent back immediately to continue in the mission field. Vimont quietly pondered the request. No missionaries had come from France in 1641 and all available priests were needed in Quebec. Even de Brébeuf, still recuperating, could not be spared, although he often asked to return to the Hurons. Vimont reluctantly agreed. He added, however, that none of the priests was available to accompany him. Instead, Vimont would ask a young *donné* named René Goupil to go with Jogues. Goupil consented wholeheartedly to make the journey and was eager to leave for the Huron country. Guillaume Coûture also chose to return.

Goupil had been enrolled in the Society of Jesus, but after the loss of some of his hearing, he decided to become a *donné*. Faithful to the goals of the Society, he vowed to pursue the aims of the Jesuits in New France and to faithfully serve the priests in the mission field. His training for hospital service would make him a great help to the priests at Sainte Marie.

They also decided that Joseph Chihwatenhwa's daughter Therese, a pupil at the overcrowded Ursuline school, should return to Ossossané. The Jesuits hoped that this pious and well-tutored thirteen-year-old would bring the word of God to her people by her example. Therese loved Mother St. Joseph and wept when she said goodbye, but she also felt happy to return to her people.

On July 28, 1642, Jogues, Goupil, Coûture, Therese, and the son of Joseph Teondechoren who had spent the winter at the Jesuit school, gathered at the shore with a number of Christian Hurons to say their farewells. Father Vimont blessed the party, and the canoes departed from Quebec laden with cloth, blankets, building materials, wheat, altar wine and vestments, as well as beads, ribbons, and gifts for the native people. The added weight of the supplies made it more difficult to maneuver the canoes through the churning waters and made the journey more dangerous.

The members of the small band, silent and attentive, felt the tension of traveling into territory where Iroquois war bands roamed. Only the splash of paddles broke the silence. As the canoes sailed on, each member of the party prayed for guidance and help. No one knew what tomorrow would bring.

CHAPTER SIX

Jogues and his party reached Three Rivers on Wednesday, July 30, arriving in time for Jogues to celebrate the feast of St. Ignatius in the chapel of the Immaculate Conception. He made his confession to Father Buteux, revealing his fears and praying for strength. Father Buteux both consoled and encouraged him. All would be well, he told Jogues, for God would decide the future.

The Jesuits received reports that the Iroquois had fled the area when they learned of the new fortifications at Richelieu. Believing the water routes were now safe, Jogues decided to press on toward Huron country immediately.

After Mass on August 1, eight more canoes joined the initial four. The party now consisted of forty people, including Eustace Ahatsistari, an important chief who spoke solemnly in a voice filled with confidence and courage.

"My brothers, if I fall into the hands of the Iroquois, I cannot hope for life. But before I die I shall taunt them. I will ask them what the white-faced Europeans bring into their country. Some axes, some kettles, some blankets, some muskets; that is all. I will tell them that the blackrobes come to us to tell us of life eternal; of a God who has made all things, of a fire that is under the earth and is prepared for all those who do not honor God. They tell us of a place of happiness in heaven, a secure place for our souls and for our bodies, which will rise once more free from suffering.... That is what I shall preach to them while they are burning me."

Charles Sondatsaa, a friend of Eustace, made a similar speech, and other Christian Hurons joined their sentiments to theirs. The words of the leaders inspired the men to greater faith and courage.

The twelve canoes sped along the waters of Lake St. Peter. The shoreline looked peaceful, the leaves on the trees glittering like silver in the bright sunlight. Birds sang while a soft breeze played among the reeds and rushes. The threat of the Iroquois seemed very distant.

Night came and they slept along the banks of the river, weapons in hand or nearby. They awoke at dawn the next day anxious to resume the journey. They quietly prepared their meager breakfast of cornmeal. Jogues assembled the little party for a brief prayer to ask God to see them safely along their way. The canoes moved out of the inlet into deeper waters, and picked up speed as they made their way through the mouth of the channel, and hugged the shore.

Suddenly one of the Hurons cried out in warning; Eustace signaled to the other canoes and each man reached for his weapon. If the Iroquois were hiding among the reeds and rushes, the party would meet them with dedicated force. Moments passed as a heavy silence hung over the canoes and the shadowy shoreline. The man who had called the warning stepped onto the sand to inspect and beckoned to the rest. He found the footprints of the Ho-de-no-sau-nee! The Iroquois had passed that way, he was certain.

Eustace turned to his companions and said, "Be they friends or enemies, it matters not; they are not in greater number than we; let us advance and fear nothing." All agreed and they settled into their canoes and cautiously made their move along the river, the water lapping softly against the shore.

Suddenly they saw bodies streaked with red paint springing from the bushes as war cries pierced the air, while the Hurons responded with their own battle cry. Mohawk warriors raised their muskets to fire. Jogues made the sign of the cross and above the din began to shout the words of absolution for his people. Jogues' canoe sped into the shoreline and crashed through a rush of tall weeds and he was thrown out. Some of the Hurons and one Frenchman abandoned their canoes and fled into the forest. Eustace, Coûture, Goupil, and a number of Hurons were caught in the foray. The Mohawks stationed farther upstream also converged on the scene and joined in the attack.

Moccasined feet passed within inches of where Jogues was hidden in the tall weeds. For a moment, he entertained the thought of remaining there until he had a chance to escape, as he later revealed:

Most assuredly I could conceal myself here among the grasses and reeds and perhaps free myself from the danger of capture. But how could I ever abandon even one of our Frenchmen, or any one of the Hurons who are already captured or who might be captured, especially those who are not baptized?... Never, never could that be. It is necessary, it must be, that my body suffer the fires of this earth to deliver these souls from the flames of hell. It must be that my body die a death that passes in order to obtain for these a life that is eternal.

Drenched from the marshy waters Jogues stood up and walked through the reeds to confront the warrior who was guarding Goupil. The man raised his weapon while three others rushed toward him, but Jogues raised his arms in surrender and called out, "Don't be frightened. Take me prisoner along with the Frenchman and the Hurons."

The suspicious warriors moved closer, and one of them struck Jogues, knocking him to the ground. Then they stripped away his black robe and dragged him off to join the other prisoners. As one of the captors prepared to tie his ankles, Jogues called out, "You don't need to bind me. These Hurons and the Frenchman are my bonds. I will not desert them. I will not leave them till death."

Jogues moved among the Hurons who lay tightly bound and spoke words of encouragement to Therese, the old men, and the two boys huddled nearby. Their eyes filled with fear. A few prisoners were non-Christian and Jogues asked if they wished to be baptized, explaining the basic beliefs of the Christian faith. When they consented, he wrung a few drops of water from his clothing to baptize them.

Shouts rose from another part of the forest, and when the crowd pushed closer Jogues grew heartsick. Eustace, the great Christian chief, had been captured. He would surely be killed, but not before being tortured. Jogues knew what awaited him and the other prisoners.

Guillaume Coûture had fought his captors with a fierceness that enabled him to escape into the forest. Coûture could easily race to freedom, but he thought of Jogues and Goupil and could not desert them. He loaded his gun and made his way back. The warriors who had pursued him appeared through a cluster of trees. As one of the men lunged at him, Coûture raised his gun and fired, but the others took up the attack and overpowered him and then dragged him back to join the other captives.

Coûture had been beaten so badly that Jogues hardly recognized his friend. When Jogues rushed to help him, he too was beaten. Jogues fell to the ground in a faint. As Goupil witnessed the punishment, he cried out, only to receive the same treatment. The Mohawks despised the French even more than the Hurons.

Several hours passed before the warriors began to celebrate their victory. It was a great day for they had captured Ondessonk, two Frenchmen, the Huron Chief Eustace Ahatsistari, and his men—twenty-three captives in all. The Bear clan had also plundered the supplies from Quebec, which they would use to good advantage. Now the prisoners awaited their transport to Iroquois villages where they expected to be tortured and killed. Jogues could barely stand, yet he moved among the captives, praying and encouraging them. Eustace and his men stood silently; the enemy would not see fear in the hearts of the courageous and strong Hurons.

Before the war party prepared the canoes for departure, they stripped a sheet of bark from a tree and in red paint sketched an image of Jogues' head, smaller heads for Therese and the three boys, and three heads in black to signify that three Hurons had been killed. Mohawks of the Bear clan preferred to transport their prisoners back to their palisades where they would undergo torture rather than killing them outright. Whoever passed this way would know that Jogues and the others had been captured and taken back to the Mohawk villages. The message would serve as a warning, a declaration that the Iroquois had conquered.

The Mohawks and their captives traveled for three days in the stifling heat, as the sun beat down on the water. His physical pain and suffering did not grieve Jogues as much as the thought of losing the Christian Hurons, the apostles for the mission. He prayed that God would give the Hurons the strength to endure the suffering that awaited them and to preserve their faith until death. He also regretted that the priests at Sainte Marie would not receive their much-needed supplies, the letters, and the books.

On the fourth day, as Jogues and Goupil traveled in the same canoe, Goupil whispered that he wished to pronounce the vows of the Society of Jesus. Jogues, filled with joy and admiration, gave his permission and accepted the vows. Then he blessed his brother in Christ.

As the days wore on, the party drew closer to the land of the Mohawks. The Christian Hurons loved and respected Ondessonk, and now they grew fonder of him as they watched him day after day ministering to them unselfishly and placing himself in danger for their sakes. Jogues grieved for all of them. When they reached Lake Champlain, they sighted a large group of Mohawk warriors on one of the islands. The captors took up a rhythmic chant, striking their paddles against the sides of their canoes and firing their muskets. When they reached the shore, they pulled the prisoners from the canoes, stripped them, and forced them to walk single file, the older men first, then the younger Hurons with Goupil and Coûture next, and lastly Ondessonk. His would be the severest punishment because he was not only French, but also a blackrobe. The captives were forced to run the gauntlet. Jogues was the last one in the long line, and appealed to a young Mohawk for a scrap of cloth to cover himself. Grudgingly the Mohawk snatched a piece of canvas from the wall and tossed it to Jogues, who secured it around his waist.

Weak from hunger and injuries, the prisoners could not run fast enough to avoid more blows from the sticks and clubs that rained on them. Coûture, instead, revived his fighting spirit and ran faster than the others, flailed his arms to protect his head, and managed to ram his elbow into the jaw of one of the Mohawk men. Enraged, the warrior beat him mercilessly.

After running the gauntlet, the captives were brought to a stage-like structure where they received more injuries from knives and stones. Many had their fingernails torn out or had their fingers, or segments of them, severed from their hands. If their wounds bled too profusely, as was the case for Goupil, they were cauterized, which only increased the agony. Hot irons were used to poke and prod Coûture's already flayed body. Jogues lay bound and helpless as burning coals were tossed at him. Each of the Hurons endured similar punishments. Jogues continued to pray for his co-workers and encourage the Hurons to remain steadfast in their faith.

When the ordeal finally ended, the captives were roped to one another and they began their journey to the village of Ossernenon (present-day Auriesville), along the banks of the Mohawk River. They were forced to run and stumbled frequently because of the pace. Jogues could not keep up and he stopped repeatedly. This so angered the Mohawks that Jogues feared that his companions might suffer because of him. He would not endanger his friends and Huron brothers; with heroic determination, he drove himself forward. They traveled for almost two weeks and reached the village on August 14, the eve of the Assumption.

By the time they reached Ossernenon, the stage for torture had already been constructed. Their agony would begin anew; Jogues suffered his own as well as that of the others. He continued to minister, console, and encourage. After the torments at Ossernenon, the captives were brought to the village of Andagaron and then Tionontoguen. The villagers realized that the men could not survive much more in their weakened condition, so they were hoisted onto the stage and left to suffer the heat and insects.

Jogues alone was dragged to the entrance of a cabin and his elbows fastened to a crossbeam and suspended. His muscles wrenched under his weight and the intense pain caused him to beg to be released. Instead, the ropes were tightened and Jogues fell unconscious. Later, he wrote:

I believed that I was going to be burned to death, for they usually act in this way when they intend to burn a prisoner. I realized that, if thus far I had endured the torments bravely and patiently, the strength and patience did not come from myself, but from God who gives courage to the afflicted. In this torture, being left, as it were to myself, I wept. Freely I glory in my infirmity so that the virtue of Christ may reside in me…. I offer thanks to you, my Lord Jesus, that I was allowed to learn by some slight experience how much you deigned to suffer for me on the cross, since the whole weight of your most sacred body hung, not from ropes, but from your hands and feet pierced with hard nails.

After Jogues regained consciousness, he learned that a visitor from a nation in the south had witnessed his suffering and had asked the Mohawks to cut their prisoner down. The law of hospitality dictated honoring a visitor's request, thus they cut the ropes. Jogues spent a pain-racked night in a longhouse.

In the morning, the prisoners were once again hauled onto the platform, but were soon forgotten. A war party was returning with new Huron captives. Jogues made his way over to them to offer words of encouragement. He hoped to baptize them before they were tortured and put to death. When he learned that two of them were to die that evening, he gathered a few drops of water that had accumulated on some cornhusks nearby, and administered baptism. The Mohawks who knew what Jogues was doing threatened to have him burned along with the Hurons.

The next day it was announced that both the great Ondessonk and Goupil would die after the ceremonial tortures were completed. Jogues spent much of his time with the Christian Hurons, comforting them and assuring them that heaven would be theirs. One of the Mohawks, convinced that Ondessonk was going about the people casting spells, dealt him a blow to the head that sent Jogues to his knees. He stayed in that position, bowed low, head in his hands. Thinking he was too weak to rise, the Mohawk left. Jogues, instead, remained there praying, assuring himself that soon he would be with his Savior.

CHAPTER SEVEN

The chiefs of the nations delayed the deaths of Jogues and his companions until they could meet in council to discuss the matter more thoroughly. Then, about three weeks after their capture, it was announced that Jogues would die the following night. Others would die with him, but their names were not yet revealed. Jogues later wrote:

Although that final act held something of horror, freedom from sin made this final act more a cause for joy. I addressed my French and Huron companions for the last time. I begged them to be of good courage. I told them to remember, amid their sufferings of body and soul, Jesus who had endured such opposition of sinners against himself. I encouraged them not to be weary, fainting in their minds, so that they should not weaken when they felt their sorrow slipping from them. Let them have hope, because tomorrow would bring us to our Lord, to reign for ever and ever. Since we feared that we would be taken away one from the other, I forewarned them, especially Eustace, as follows: since we would not be able to be close together, each one should look toward me; when he lifted his hand to his heart and raised his eyes to heaven, he would thus give testimony that he was sorry for his sins. Then I would impart absolution to him, as I had often done on the road down and since our arrival.

The next morning passed, and in the afternoon word spread that no one would die that night. Some of the chiefs opposed the death verdict, and the chiefs and sachems were meeting again to decide what to do with their captives. The warring faction wanted to exterminate the French, Algonquins, and Hurons. Other more powerful chiefs wanted a wiser policy, one that promoted amicable relations with the French. Peace offers had failed in the past, but the murder of Ondessonk and the two Frenchmen would shatter any prospects of an alliance. Ondessonk and the two others could easily be held hostage indefinitely or traded to the native's advantage. Jogues and his companions whispered their prayers and awaited the outcome.

The meeting had ended late that evening. Jogues and Goupil were brought to the chief's cabin. He announced that they would return to the village of Ossernenon and remain there as his slaves. Ihandich (Coûture) would remain at Tionontoguen as a slave in the cabin of the chief he had slain. Eustace Ahatsistari would be burned at Tionontoguen, but Stephen would belong to the people of Andagaron. Paul Onnonhoaraton, the nephew of Eustace, would be offered as a sacrifice at Ossernenon. All the other Hurons would be assigned to families who would decide their fate: slavery, adoption, or death.

Jogues was stunned. Eustace Ahatsistari, the courageous Huron chief and exemplary Christian would be put to death! Stephen and Paul were also to die. It seemed that with them would die any hope for more conversions among the Hurons.

Goupil and Jogues had been granted a reprieve. They rejoiced at the possibility that they might find opportunities to pray together, to speak of spiritual realities, and to encourage one another. Their days, however, were filled with chores and duties, many of which proved too difficult for them in their malnourished condition. Nonetheless, they offered their days to God and did what was expected of them as best they could.

As he went about his tasks, Goupil often lifted his eyes to heaven, moving his lips in silent prayer. This angered an old man who lived in the cabin. He believed that Goupil was calling upon demons. Aware of the people's fears, Jogues cautioned his friend against this, but Goupil continued out of habit. He loved children, and on one occasion traced the sign of the cross on a child—an act the old man witnessed with silent hatred.

On September 29, 1642, while Jogues and Goupil were walking in the shade of the pine forest praying the rosary, two young men came to tell them that they were to return to the house. "I had some premonition of what was going to happen," Jogues wrote in a later account. He said to Goupil, "Let us commend ourselves to God and to our good Mother, Mary. I think these people have some evil plan."

As they approached the gate to the village, one of the men drew out a hatchet he had been concealing and brought it down on Goupil's head. His body crumpled to the ground, the name of Jesus on his lips. Seeing the bloodied weapon, Jogues readied himself, expecting to receive the same. When he realized that his friend was still alive, he gave him final absolution and embraced his body as the warriors delivered two more blows to Goupil's head. Jogues was sent back to his cabin and Goupil's limp body was dragged into the woods.

Jogues was heartsick. He begged God to give him strength. Dear, gentle René, innocent and steadfast in his faith, did not deserve this fate. Jogues, however, was consoled by the fact that his brother and companion was already in heaven at peace in the company of the Father among the army of martyrs.

Jogues was now confined to his cabin, but he was determined to find Goupil's body and bury it, no matter what the cost. A few Mohawks wanted to protect him and they tried to discourage him, but on the third day after Goupil's death, he slipped away. Jogues headed toward the forest path where his friend had been murdered. The ground still had signs of the direction in which the body had been dragged. This led Jogues and an Algonquin companion to the river's edge. They searched among the reeds and Jogues waded through the shallow, cold waters to look around the tall grass. Then they spied Goupil's body caught in the gnarled roots of a tree.

Tenderly, Jogues picked up the body and looked quickly for a place to hide it until he could bury it. With the help of the Algonquin, he placed the body beneath the surface of the stream and weighed it down with large stones so no one would find it. Jogues intended to return with a pickax the next day in order to dig a grave for the body. A full day passed before he could return. The river had swollen from heavy rains and when Jogues came to the place where he had arranged the stones, he could not find Goupil's body. Thinking that the body may have been dislodged and carried downstream, he entered the ice-cold waters. Finding nothing, Jogues returned to the village with a saddened heart. He later learned that some of the young men of the village had found the body and dragged it into the nearby woods to leave for the animals.

After the winter snows had melted, Jogues learned from some of the villagers that he would soon be brought back to Three Rivers. Jogues could not leave without looking for Goupil's remains. After he searched the woods a number of times, he at last found some of the bones, which he buried with the intention of taking them with him to Three Rivers.

Jogues sent an account of Goupil's death to his Jesuit superiors. He told of Goupil's entrance into the Society of Jesus despite his ill health, and of his purpose and desire to live for God, especially in New France. He was a gifted surgeon and he tended the sick in Quebec. "He left so sweet an aroma of his goodness and his other virtues in that place that his memory is still held in benediction there." Jogues wrote of Goupil's joy over being chosen for the mission to the Hurons, of his edifying conversations along the trail, of his request to profess vows as a coadjutor in the Society. He described Goupil's respectful treatment of the native people, his refusal to escape the Mohawks, and how he died making the sign of the cross. Jogues recounted his search for Goupil's body in order to bury it, how he had found the remaining bones and "kissed them very devoutly several times, as the bones of a martyr of Jesus Christ. I give him this title, not only because he was killed…in the exercise of an ardent charity toward his neighbor—for he placed himself in evident peril for the love of God—but especially because he was killed on account of prayer and notably, for the sake of the holy cross."

Without Goupil, Jogues felt more isolated than ever, but he continued to do whatever good he was able. During his stay at the village, Jogues had been given the most menial and strenuous tasks, yet he bore all mistreatment with patience and courage. He would sometimes retreat into the forest, to a large tree where he had carved a cross into the bark, and there he would spend time in prayer. Because he had not tried to escape, he was given more and more freedom to move about. He traveled from one village to another to minister to the Christian Hurons whom the Mohawks had taken prisoner.

In July 1643, his captors took Jogues with them on a fishing trip about twenty miles below Fort Orange. Some of the men decided to canoe farther up the river to the settlement of Rensselaerswyck to trade with the Dutch, and they took Jogues with them.

The population of Rensselaerswyck numbered about 100 farmers and tenants of Van Rensselaer, the *patroon* or proprietor. About thirty wooden, thatch-roofed houses had been erected near the shores of the Hudson River. While the Mohawks did their trading, Jogues conversed with the settlers. He learned that the Dutch had unsuccessfully attempted to gain his release. He also learned that his captors were planning to kill him when he returned to the village. A war party of Mohawks had recently set out for the French colony, intending to destroy it. Jogues wanted to warn the French; he obtained pen and paper and wrote a hasty letter to his superior in the Huron language, as well as in French and Latin.

Van Corlaer, an influential Dutch settler who had attempted to free Jogues, strongly urged the priest to escape. He offered passage on a Dutch ship that would soon sail for Rochelle. Jogues thanked his benefactor, but asked to delay his decision for the night so that he might pray for God's guidance. He was tormented with questions and doubt. Would he be shirking his duties and responsibilities to souls if he escaped? If he returned only to be killed, would it not be suicide? And what of Coûture who had refused to escape as long as Jogues remained captive? If he escaped, then Coûture could find his way to freedom. In the morning, confident about his decision, he returned to the Dutch and told them he would accept their offer. They told Jogues that a small boat would be waiting on the shore, and when the opportunity presented itself, he was to row out to the waiting vessel.

Evening came and Jogues lodged in a barn with the Mohawks, who slept quite soundly with the help of the Dutch's supply of rum. Silently, Jogues crept through the darkness. Outside the barn, he heard a low growl and then hot pain coursed through his leg. One of the farmer's dogs had bitten him. He hobbled back into the barn, where the pain kept him awake all night. Toward morning, a servant of the Dutch farmer came to the barn. Jogues motioned him to silence the dogs. The man understood at once, led him from the barn, and directed him to the shore where the small boat was waiting. With great effort, Jogues struggled to push the boat out into the water. He rowed to the vessel where the sailors welcomed him and stowed him down in the hold, placing a large chest over the hatchway. Jogues remained in that suffocating atmosphere for two sweltering days and nights.

On the second night, the Minister of the Dutch came to tell Jogues that the Mohawks were creating a great disturbance over his disappearance. The settlers were growing fearful that the Mohawks would set fire to their town. Jogues said he had no desire to escape at the expense of the people, so he made plans to return to shore. The sailors who had promised him security and safe passage were offended, but Jogues finally convinced them to allow him to return to shore and go to the home of the commandant of the Dutch fort.

The commandant hid Jogues in the attic of a nearby house for all of August and most of September. He suffered in the hot, cramped quarters, and had little to eat and drink. Finally, toward the end of September, the Dutch satisfied the Mohawks with a large ransom. Jogues was then placed aboard a vessel bound for Manhattan, and sent to the governor in charge of the whole territory of New Amsterdam. Jogues was received kindly and given clothes and passage aboard a vessel bound for England. He arrived at the port of Falmouth the day before Christmas, then obtained passage on a coal ship bound for Brittany. He made his way ashore not far from Brest on Christmas day, just in time to celebrate Mass.

January 5, 1644, was a day like no other. A merchant had befriended Jogues, and at his own expense, took him to Rennes. Jogues knocked at the door of the Jesuit college and asked to see the rector. The porter, seeing the woolen cap and threadbare clothes, told him that the rector was busy. Jogues asked him to please deliver a message: he had news of New France. Jogues was immediately brought into a warm parlor and seated near the crackling fire. The rector came in and questioned his visitor about the Jesuits in New France. Not recognizing him, the rector asked if he was acquainted with Father Isaac Jogues.

"I know him very well," came the reply.

"We have had word that the Iroquois have taken him prisoner," continued the rector. "Is he alive? Have they murdered him?"

"No," Jogues replied, "he is alive and at liberty. It is he who speaks to you." And he fell to his knees to receive his superior's blessing. The rector embraced Jogues and seeing his disfigured hands, took them in his own, and kissed them.

Although he was overjoyed to be in France again, Jogues' heart burned with only one desire: to return to Canada and minister to the Hurons. Would his dream ever be fulfilled?

Chapter Eight

The colonists in Quebec had appealed to France to send supplies and military personnel to protect them from Iroquois attacks. After many delays, a fleet carrying soldiers equipped with muskets and armor finally arrived in the summer of 1644. The people of New France flocked to their churches. Masses were said in thanksgiving and voices rang with joy.

From the first ship to reach Quebec, a ghost-like figure of a blackrobe with thinning red hair and a red, gray-streaked beard disembarked. His hands were greatly disfigured, with only remnants of fingers. Still, no one could mistake the peaceful look in his blue eyes. It was Isaac Jogues! He told Governor de Montmagny, Vimont, and de Brébeuf his story of how the Dutch had helped him to escape, how he had found passage on a ship to France, and how he had immediately asked to be sent back to Quebec.

The other Jesuits told Jogues how grieved they had been when they found out he had been captured. The Hurons in his party who had managed to escape soon returned to Quebec and related the events of the ambush. Then in June 1643, two emaciated Hurons arrived at Three Rivers: Joseph Teondechoren and Peter Saoekbata, Chihwatenhwa's two brothers. They had been captured with Jogues the previous summer and tortured, but had somehow managed to escape. They told the Jesuits of Goupil's death and of Jogues' enslavement, and of how greatly Therese suffered because she could not practice her faith openly. The Mohawks wanted her to marry one of their young men. Joseph warned de Brébeuf to be wary of the peace offerings of the Iroquois who planned a treacherous peace with the French with the intention of exterminating the Huron and Algonquin Nations.

De Brébeuf told Jogues how one day when he was making his rounds in the village of Three Rivers, an Iroquois strode into the settlement. They soon discovered that he was a peace envoy, and had brought a letter from Jogues to Governor de Montmagny. The tattered paper on which the letter was written was still legible. The script, written in Latin, Huron, and French, was difficult to decipher. Jogues had written:

Here is the fourth letter I have written since I am with the Iroquois. The design of the Iroquois, as far as I can see, is to capture all the Hurons. When they have put to death the more important ones and a large part of the others, they propose to make of them one people and one land.... The Dutch have tried to ransom us, but in vain.... I am resolved to dwell here as long as it shall please our Lord and not to escape, even though an opportunity should present itself.

Hoping to contact Jogues, de Brébeuf traveled to Fort Richelieu with a letter for him. The peace envoy was being held hostage at the Fort, and de Brébeuf questioned him to learn as much as he could about Jogues' situation. But the sullen envoy was unwilling to talk. In the dim light of the cabin, de Brébeuf studied the man's features and realized he had seen him before. He was a Huron whom the Iroquois had adopted. Although the "peace envoy" did not give any information, he asked to stay, for the Mohawks would kill him if he returned to them. De Brébeuf agreed to his request.

Jogues listened intently to all that had happened in Quebec during his captivity. The priests told him that Father Francois Bressani, de Brébeuf's assistant at Sillery, had asked to be sent to the Huron country, and was notified that he could make his way there as soon as conditions appeared safe. Six Hurons baptized by de Brébeuf in December had decided to make the trip with Bressani. They set out on April 27, 1644. Two days later, it was reported that the Iroquois had massacred the small company.

But in May, a gaunt, half-starved figure staggered into the settlement of Three Rivers. De Brébeuf took him in at once and tended his wounds, fed him, and made him rest. When the man was strong enough, he explained what had happened to Bressani's party. They had been fifteen miles down river when a group of Iroquois ambushed them. One Huron had been killed in the attack, and the messenger thought that Bressani had also died. Instead, Bressani had been captured, tortured, and finally sold to the Dutch, who helped him return to France. He later returned to Canada and stayed there until the destruction of the Huron mission.

Jogues shuddered, knowing all too well what Bressani had suffered. Yet, he also rejoiced to be back in Canada and even hoping to establish a mission among the Iroquois. For the time being, he was assigned to Montreal.

De Brébeuf wanted to return to Sainte Marie. Father Vimont gave his consent, and de Brébeuf left for Huronia at the end of the summer of 1644. The crisp winds of early autumn blew through the trees along the riverbank as they paddled their canoes toward Sainte Marie. Finally, thirty days after their departure, they spotted the familiar shoreline of the Hurons' homeland. De Brébeuf rose from his cramped position in the canoe to hear the voices that came from the tree line, voices he recognized, French voices.

De Brébeuf shifted his weight, and before the canoe could come ashore, he was wading out into the shallow water. Even as he stepped onto the shore, he was in the arms of his comrades. De Brébeuf, the most loved of all the priests, had come home! In the timbered chapel, the *donnés*, the *engages*, and the missioners sang the *Te Deum* in thanksgiving to God for the safe arrival of their beloved brother.

Joyous laughter rippled through the common room, alternating with a quiet exchange of questions and answers. No, de Brébeuf had not encountered any Iroquois; yes, new missioners would arrive soon in the persons of Noël Chabanel and Leonard Garreau accompanied by twenty-two French soldiers.

In Father Jerome Lalemant's private study, de Brébeuf presented the documents sent by Father Vimont informing Lalemant of his appointment as superior of the mission of New France. Paul Ragueneau would take his place as superior of the Huron mission. Lalemant accepted his new appointment in a spirit of obedience, though he would not be able to travel to Quebec until the following spring.

The other missioners were happy with the choice of Ragueneau. He was much like de Brébeuf, and indeed had patterned himself after the admired priest. He was warm, outgoing, understanding, and caring, besides being prayerful and intelligent. The Hurons called him "Aondechate," and the esteem they had for him matched that for de Brébeuf. Charles Garnier wrote of Ragueneau: "No one seems to be more worthy of the appointment to his office than Father Paul Ragueneau, since he is endowed with extraordinary gifts of virtue, talent, prudence, and learning."

Fourteen priests resided at Sainte Marie that winter, along with two Jesuit lay brothers, eleven *donnés*, nine workmen, and twenty-two soldiers, so that feeding and housing the many Frenchmen did not pose a problem. The large vegetable gardens they had planted had yielded an abundant harvest. The livestock they had brought from Quebec were thriving. The compound housed residences, a hospital, storage, workrooms, and a chapel. The fortress itself resembled a bit of old France, while some of the structures were built in the style of the Huron longhouses. On a hill, a cemetery waited to receive Christian burials.

Overjoyed that their Echon had returned, the Hurons converged upon Sainte Marie to welcome him. De Brébeuf, filled with love for his brethren, responded in kind.

The appointments for the coming year sent Garnier to Teanaustayé. Father Menard would accompany him and minister to the Algonquins. De Brébeuf would remain at Sainte Marie and take charge of five neighboring villages. Ragueneau would live at Ossossané. Chaumonot and Du Peron were sent to Scanonaenrat and St. Ignace, while Daniel and Le Moyne were assigned the frontier village of Cahiagué. The priests maintained their own cabins in the villages, but returned now and then to Sainte Marie, their headquarters or "home."

The Iroquois threat still hung over the Hurons and the Algonquins, though a tenuous peace with the Senecas had been implemented that winter. Famine, a frequent problem during the winter, also threatened the Huron villagers, who looked to the spring and to Sainte Marie for food.

When the rivers had thawed sufficiently to allow for travel, Lalemant left for Quebec with sixty canoes of Huron traders taking their pelts to New France. The soldiers departed as well and since they had actually proved a nuisance, de Brébeuf was relieved to see them go.

Sainte Marie bustled with renewed activity. The Frenchmen had to plant crops, put up new buildings, and repair old structures. Chickens wandered about in the yard, cows grazed in the pastures, and pigs roamed about their pens. The summer wore on, turning into a hot and humid August. The Huron women went to the fields early in the morning to avoid the heat, while the older men sat in the shade and told stories of the past. The young men stalked the forests for any sign of the Iroquois, while the chiefs smoked their pipes in longhouses and tried to anticipate their enemies' next move.

Meanwhile, de Brébeuf made his annual spiritual exercises. "Every day from now on, at the time of Communion, with the consent of the superior, I will vow that I will do whatever I shall know to be for the greater glory of God and for his greater service. The conditions of this vow are twofold: (1) I, myself, when the matter appears properly, clearly, and without doubt, will judge a thing to be for the greater glory of God; (2) If there appear some doubt, I shall consult the superior or spiritual father."

De Brébeuf's spirit moved to greater heights, and he often confided in his superior, Father Ragueneau, who later wrote:

He derived his spirit of confidence in God from prayer, in which he was often much uplifted. A single word would give him a theme for whole hours—not to his intellect, of whose inaction he was wont to complain—but to his heart, which relished the eternal truths of faith and which remained attached to them with serenity, love, and joy.

The hot spell continued into September, and though no one from Quebec was expected, one day a canoe slid onto the shore of Sainte Marie. De Brébeuf and the missioners found Father Francois Bressani on their doorstep.

After a joyous and rather boisterous welcome, Bressani spoke about his experience with the Iroquois and how they had tortured him and threatened his life many times. He had made no converts during his stay with them, but he had baptized a Huron catechumen about to be burned at the stake. He explained that this had enraged the Iroquois, who then bound

Bressani so tightly that he had asked them to loosen his bonds. This request was sometimes honored, but only if the guard and Bressani were alone so that no one else could witness this act of kindness.

In silent awe, de Brébeuf noted the scars that covered Bressani's face, neck, and arms, and his maimed hands. A strong desire to join the ranks of the martyrs welled up in de Brébeuf's heart. As he looked into Bressani's eyes, he saw a light burning, a desire to suffer anew for Jesus; he understood then that his own desire would be fulfilled. He could see the stake, the flames, the fire. He could see his own blood being shed for Jesus Christ.

News from Quebec came with the first spring thaw. In January 1646, Father Anne de Noüe had left Three Rivers for the French fort at the mouth of the Richelieu River. There he would offer Mass and hear confessions. Although he had come to New France twenty-one years earlier, de Noüe had not mastered the native languages, but with the help of an interpreter he tended the spiritual needs of his flock. He also cared for the sick, and fished and gathered food to distribute to the people. But de Noüe was now sixty-three years old and the trip to Richelieu in the coldest month of the year had proved disastrous for him.

The priest, two soldiers, and one Huron set out on snowshoes. The soldiers pulled sleds piled high with baggage, making their way along the trail. Deep snow lay high on the shores of the St. Lawrence River and in the forests, but the party managed to travel eighteen miles the first day. Unfamiliar with snowshoes, the soldiers grew weary. They camped in the forest, in dugouts of snow, lighting a fire within the center of the barricade, and then fell asleep.

During the night, Father de Noüe awoke to moonlight as bright as day. He knew the way to Richelieu very well, having traveled it many times. Why not go alone, he thought, and send a party back to help the weary soldiers with their sleds? They would have no difficulty, he reasoned, following the prints of his snowshoes the next morning. Because he was certain that he would arrive at the fort by the following night, he only took a few prunes and bread as he started out. By mid-morning, however, the sky had turned ominously gray. A cold wind began to blow, and thick snow fell relentlessly on the darkened path. Father de Nouë lost his way, circling and re-tracing his steps all day. Night came and he burrowed into the deep snow, sleeping without a cover or a fire.

When the soldiers and the Huron awoke, the storm had erased all trace of de Nouë's tracks, and before long, they, too, lost their way. They camped for the night in a spot not far from where the priest lay, on the shore of the Island of St. Ignace. More fully aware of the danger of the situation than the soldiers, the Huron decided to press on alone. Before long, he sighted the small fort in the heart of its snowcapped palisades. He asked for de Nouë, and everyone realized that the priest must be somewhere out in the snow, lost and alone, they could do nothing until morning.

The two soldiers were rescued the next day, but Father de Nouë could not be found. The search party combed the area, shouting and firing muskets in the hope that de Nouë would hear and respond. The echo of French voices and firearms resounded, but de Nouë did not answer.

A French soldier and a Christian Huron named Charles continued the search the following day. The sharp instinct and trained eyes of the Huron noted the slight depressions where snow had covered de Nouë's tracks. They followed the prints and found the camp, not far from the fort. The priest had come within sight of the fort, but had failed to see it.

Saints Jean de la Lande, Isaac Jogues and René Goupil
(courtesy of Auriesville shrine).

Artist's rendition of the martyrs in glory (courtesy of Auriesville shrine).

The most accurate representation of Isaac Jogues, taken from a portrait possessed by his niece (courtesy of Auriesville shrine).

Sketch based on the above portrait, with signature taken from the Jesuit Relations *(courtesy of Auriesville shrine).*

Portraits of the eight martyrs
(courtesy of Midland shrine):

St. John de Brébeuf

St. Gabriel Lalemant

St. Noël Chabanel

St. Anthony Daniel

St. Jean de la Lande, St. René Goupil

St. Charles Garnier

St. Isaac Jogues

The path leading to the ravine where Isaac Jogues attempted to bury the body of René Goupil (courtesy of Auriesville shrine).

"Theresa's Rosary" at Auriesville, which commemorates the Algonquin woman who used a path made of stones as a makeshift rosary during her captivity at Ossernenon (courtesy of Auriesville shrine).

*The Martyrs' Shrine at Midland, Ontario
(courtesy of Joseph Newman, SJ).*

The Martyrs' Shrine at Auriesville, New York
(courtesy of Auriesville shrine).

premiere meditation
Du soing de l'aduancement spirituel

A meditation written by Gabriel Lalemant at Sainte Marie and preserved by Paul Ragueneau (courtesy of Midland shrine).

*Aerial view of the mission at Sainte Marie [1639–1649]
(courtesy of Midland shrine).*

Ego Antonius Daniel,
professionem facio, & promitto
Apud Hurones in noua Francia
Die vicesimo Septimo Septembris...

Antonius Daniel

On September 27, 1640, St. Anthony Daniel made his profession of
vows as a Jesuit for the mission among the Hurons in New France
(courtesy of Midland shrine).

SAINT ISAAC JOGUES. PRIEZ POUR NOUS

A memorial to St. Isaac Jogues at a Jesuit church
in Quebec (courtesy of Midland shrine).

*A monument to the martyrs at St. Michael's Church
in Sillery, Quebec (courtesy of Midland shrine).*

Map of New France (courtesy of Yale University Press).

Map of New France

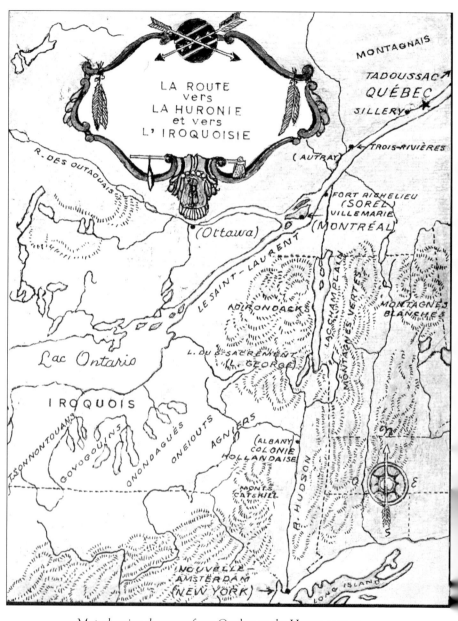

Map showing the route from Quebec to the Huron country
(courtesy of Midland shrine).

The men found de Noüe in the center of the hollowed out patch of snow he had dug. He was kneeling on the icy earth, hat and snowshoes at his side. His hands were clasped to his breast and his face turned looking up to heaven. His body was nearly frozen, but he had somehow survived.

The harsh climate was not the only threat the missionaries faced. The Iroquois seemed to become bolder with each victory. They stalked the Huron route from the Lower Ottawa to Three Rivers, hunting Algonquins and Hurons. No one was safe.

CHAPTER NINE

In May 1645, Governor Montmagny of Quebec sent an Iroquois prisoner back to his people with the promise to release two more if the Iroquois would agree to peace. They responded by sending a small group of envoys to the French, and talks were held in July. Dressed in native fashion, Guillaume Coûture, who the Iroquois had adopted, served as interpreter. Although two years had already passed since they had parted in the Mohawk country, Jogues recognized him immediately and ran to embrace him.

Kiotseaeton, leader of the Mohawk delegation, wore the traditional beaded skins and feathers. He was known as an eloquent speaker, and his ambassadors, Aniwogan and Tokhrahenehiaron, possessed the same gift with the addition of movements that made them appear as actors on a stage. Jogues knew these men very well; they had been instrumental in having him tortured two years before. Now, they avoided meeting his eyes. Jogues amazed them with a warm welcome, taking their hands in his without a trace of animosity or reproach. Kiotseaeton and Coûture proclaimed their intense loyalty to the French. Kiotseaeton expressed his sorrow over the refusal of the other four nations to participate in the discussion, but he emphasized his conviction that it would be only a matter of time before they, too, agreed to make peace.

In the dim light of the cabin at Three Rivers, Governor Montmagny listened attentively to the words of the envoy. The Algonquins, faces and bodies painted white to signify peace, wore headdresses of bright feathers. The Mohawks also wore their finest headdresses and buckskin jackets decorated with colored beads and quills. In their arms and over their shoulders they supported heavy wampum belts, gifts to show their sincerity. In contrast, wearing their plain black robes, the Jesuits quietly awaited the outcome.

The parties exchanged the beaded belts. Eloquent speeches and promises of peace were delivered. The Mohawk ambassadors were honored, feasted, and entertained in the company of Governor Montmagny; Vimont, superior of the mission; the Jesuits-in-residence; and the enemy tribes. The Algonquins, the Montagnais, the Attikamègues, and the Hurons all sat together. The Mohawks, however, insisted upon being seated near the French—an act they claimed was a sign of their affection and respect for the French. Two poles had been planted in the ground and a line stretched between them on which the wampum belts were hung. The envoys sang the song of peace and presented the wampum; the ornate beads on each belt symbolized some aspect of the events that had finally led to peace.

Kiotseaeton profusely expressed his desire for peace. He even spoke kindly to the Hurons, presented gifts, thanked them for the courtesy they had shown to prisoners, and asked for their release. He was evasive when asked about including the Algonquins in the peace treaty. However, he vowed to send ambassadors to the Huron nation as a gesture of friendship and peace. At the same time, he warned that the other Iroquois tribes might not accept the peace.

The exclusion of the Algonquins from the peace proceedings distressed Governor Montmagny who discussed ways to resolve this issue with his advisors and Father Lalemant. It was decided that the French would agree to the peace if the Christian Algonquins were included in the treaty. For now, the non-Christian Algonquins would be excluded.

Further talks were held in September 1645 and in February 1646. Father Jogues' knowledge of the Mohawk's life and culture made him an invaluable participant. Kiotseaeton assured Jogues that he would be welcome in Ossernenon if he would honor the Mohawks with his return. Jogues was elated. Although the Jesuits hoped for a lasting peace that would further their missionary efforts in the New World, they could not suppress their fear and doubt. The long-time enemy of the French, the Mohawks alone had asked for peace and without the consent of the other four nations. The Senecas, Onondagas, Cayugas, and Oneidas continued their attacks against the French and natives at Montreal, as well as against the Hurons, Algonquins, and other vulnerable tribes. Still, Montmagny, the colonists, and the Jesuits were anxious to pursue peace with the Mohawks.

Coûture willingly agreed to return with the members of the peace envoy to their villages and to spend the remainder of the winter among the Mohawks in the hope of binding them to their promises. The French deliberated privately. They decided that someone whose reputation the natives esteemed should return as well; Jogues would be the perfect ambassador. He knew the language and the characteristics of the Iroquois people. He would have a twofold mission: first political, in that he would bring gifts to cement relations—wampum belts from Governor Montmagny to show good faith; secondly, and more importantly, his mission would be religious. He would establish a new mission, the Mission of the Martyrs.

Jogues had lived at Montreal for two years, but his disfigured hands were a constant reminder of what he had experienced. The scars were not only physical; he suffered mental anguish as well. The tortures he had endured returned to him in the form of nightmares, from which he awoke bathed in sweat. Although Jogues yearned to return to the Mohawks, the thought of returning evoked fear, hesitation, and aversion. He prayed for strength and guidance, and eventually the feelings passed. He would willingly accept his role as peace ambassador if chosen. He asked God to find him worthy to return to the Mohawks.

Jogues dispatched a letter to his new superior, Lalemant, in which he offered himself as a missionary to the Iroquois people. Jogues prayed that he would receive an affirmative reply by May, when the Great Council would be held then at Three Rivers.

Jogues and Coûture, eager to discuss their adventures in captivity, sat before a crackling fire and reminisced. Coûture told Jogues that he felt he had lost some of his dedication during his stay among the Mohawks, while Jogues spoke of his desire to return. In the end, Jogues approved of the faithful *donné's* desire to be released from his vows. Guillaume was free to remain in Quebec, and he now wanted to settle there and marry. Jogues urged his friend to petition Lalemant, making his desires known, just as he had in the letter Coûture would deliver. Jogues prayed both petitions would be granted.

Father Lalemant pondered the two decisions and discussed them with his advisors. In his journal for April 26, 1646, he noted, "I held a consultation with reference to Father Jogues' journey to the Anniehronnons (Mohawks).... The decision was absolute. Coûture was free to remain with the French and marry, as he desired. Jogues was bound anew, as was his wish, to serve God and his superiors in poverty, chastity, and obedience, within the Mohawk villages, until death claimed him."

The Great Council convened at Three Rivers in May as planned. The St. Lawrence flowed again with the rhythm of the new season as Kiotseaeton and his envoys came up from their country to present gifts to Montmagny. Again, Coûture was chosen to represent the French. As an adopted son and member of the Mohawk family, he would be useful as a skilled peace ambassador to the Mohawks.

Coûture offered a necklace that contained a thousand beads. It was promised that the hearths of Three Rivers would be kept warm for the Mohawks, who were welcome to come at any time. Paul Teswahat, an Algonquin chief, spoke for all the Algonquin Nations. He presented the Mohawks with elk skins, proclaiming that the Algonquins had thrown their hatchets away and that Algonquin land was open to the Mohawks whenever they wished to hunt or fish.

Montmagny pledged to send two Frenchmen to the Mohawks to cement the bond of peace between them and the French. These would be Father Jogues, who knew their language and customs, and the notable French advisor, Jean Bourdon. They would depart for the Mohawk villages at the end of May. Gifts were offered as well. The peace hinged upon Kiotseaeton's acceptance. Lalemant and Montmagny waited in the dimly lit cabin. Finally the answer came. Kiotseaeton not only accepted the proposition, but also guaranteed safety to the ambassadors. The Algonquins offered to send two of their own envoys, and the pact was sealed.

During this time, Jogues was making his annual spiritual exercises, and for ten days isolated himself and prayed. One day a gentle rapping at the door interrupted him. It was Father Le Jeune. Silently, his face devoid of expression, he handed Jogues the long-awaited letter from Lalemant. Asking God for strength to accept whatever decision Lalemant had made, Jogues opened the envelope and read the brief note. Jogues was instructed to be ready as soon as possible to return to the Mohawks.

Ten years earlier, when Jogues was at Rouen preparing to sail to Canada, he had offered himself totally to God. Now he did so again, using the prayer St. Ignatius had composed: "Take, O Lord, and receive all my liberty, my memory, my understanding and all my will, whatever I have and possess. You have given all these things to me; to you, O Lord, I restore them; all are yours; dispose of them according to your will. Give me your love and your grace, for this is enough for me."

He quickly replied to Lalemant:

Most Reverend and dear Father:

Your letter found me engaged in the exercises of my retreat, which I began after the departure of the canoe that carried my letter to you. It was a good time, for the Indians are all away on the chase and give us more silence. Would you believe me that, when I opened the letter, my heart at first was seized as if with dread? I feared that that which I desired and that which my spirit would prize as the greatest of all desires, might actually come to pass. My poor nature, which remembered all that had gone before, trembled. But our Lord, in his goodness, bestowed calm on it and will calm it still more. Yes, Father, I desire all that our Lord desires and I desire it at the peril of a thousand lives. Ah, with what regret should I be filled, if I lost such a wonderful occasion, one on which it might depend only on me that some souls were not saved.... I owe you the account of the capture and death of our good René Goupil, which I should already have sent to you.... If God wills that I go to the Iroquois, it is necessary that he who accompanies me must be virtuous, docile, courageous, one who would be willing to suffer any-thing for God, one who is able to make and handle canoes, so that, independently of the Indians, we might be able to go and come. Permit me to send my respects to our reverend fathers. I am your humble and obedient servant.

Isaac Jogues, from Montreal, the 2nd of May, 1646.

Jogues immediately prepared for the journey and left Three Rivers. On the advice of an Algonquin sage, he wore a doublet and hose rather than his black robe. His superior agreed that

Jogues would be more favorably received if he were not dressed as a cleric. He was accompanied by Jean Bourdon, engineer to the governor, two Algonquins and four Mohawks. The priest brought a quantity of gifts with which to confirm the peace. They borrowed canoes at a fishing station and proceeded to Fort Orange, where Jogues encountered those who had saved his life. The Dutch were pleased to see their friend alive and well, but Jogues, though he enjoyed seeing these kind people, was anxious to embark upon his mission. Two days later, he departed for the Mohawk villages.

As Jogues drew closer to Ossernenon, his pulse throbbed and his heart quickened. Memories of the pain and suffering he had endured there gnawed at his spirit. Yet as the sun shone brightly and summer transfigured the land, the thought of the new mission warmed and calmed him.

Upon his arrival, a council was held in the dark interior of a smoky longhouse. Jogues presented the gifts and relayed the messages of peace from Governor Montmagny. The chiefs smoked their pipes and nodded in silence. The Algonquin gifts met a cold reception, and Jogues realized the fragility of the peace.

The chiefs conferred over the important decisions they were about to make. They accepted the gifts, the wampum, and the good wishes of the French, but urged Jogues to return home quickly. They said that if the other four nations learned of his presence, he and his envoys, the Algonquins, would surely be killed. Jogues prayed long into the star-filled night, pondering the decision to leave, asking God to guide his judgment. He decided that his return to Canada would spare the Algonquins' lives and secure the peace. He must heed the Mohawks' warning and go back to New France. He made the rounds of the cabins in the morning, hearing the confessions of the native converts and instructing a number of Christian prisoners.

Jogues had a small black chest that contained personal items. He decided to leave the box with his "aunt" in the longhouse of the family who had adopted him during his days as a slave. Because the Mohawks believed the box contained evil charms or some sinister secrets, Jogues displayed the contents: a book, some wax, and a few articles of clothing. Thinking he had dispelled their fears, he locked the box and promised to return to retrieve it.

The completion of their diplomatic mission left Jogues and Jean Bourdon free to return to Quebec. Yet, a vision of the new Mission of the Martyrs remained in Jogues' heart and mind. He could only hope that his dream of establishing a mission among the Iroquois Nations would become a reality.

The peace between the French and the Mohawks was tenuous; progress, no matter how little, had to be preserved at all costs. In late August, Lalemant again appointed Jogues as a peace envoy to the Mohawks.

Lalemant later wrote, "Father Jogues was ready sooner than the proposition was made to him." He who had sustained the dangers of war was not one to retreat in time of peace. He was welcomed among the Iroquois people and glad to sound out their friendship after having experienced their enmity. He was also aware that they could change their attitude at any moment and he understood the danger.

Jogues had just three days to get ready. He took special care in arranging candles, wine, a small chalice, an altar cloth, a missal, and hosts in a small trunk. Although he desired this mission, Jogues had a sense of foreboding. Before departing he wrote to a friend, "I shall go and shall not return." Despite his sense of imminent danger, he felt a peace he had never known before.

On the morning of September 24, 1646, Jogues departed for the Mohawk village along with a *donné*, Jean de la Lande, who had been chosen for his fine qualities. Jogues warned him of the dangers they would face, but the young man said he was ready to undertake the mission. Jogues wrote that de la Lande had "declared that the desire to serve God drew him to a land where he fully expected to meet his death."

The canoes set out in early morning. Jogues, Jean de la Lande, and Otrihouré (a Huron who was now an Iroquois) traveled in one canoe. Three Hurons who desired to visit relatives—prisoners of the Mohawks—followed in another canoe. Some Mohawks who were returning home trailed in a third canoe. On this trip Jogues decided to dress in his familiar black robe. His mission was primarily a mission for God, one to evangelize the Mohawks.

When the party reached the mouth of the Richelieu River, the Hurons decided to return to their own country after hearing that Iroquois were attacking Huron villages and hunting down any who escaped. The Mohawks pressed on ahead. Jogues, de la Lande, and Otrihouré continued the trip alone.

The trees cast shadows on the orange and red leaf-covered path. Jogues was in high spirits as he instructed de la Lande on the proper conduct among the Mohawks, cautioned him about certain ways of acting, and warned him of the worst that could happen. The closer they moved to Ossernenon, the village Jogues had christened "Holy Trinity," the more enthusiastic he became about the new mission he was to establish among the Mohawks. When he had departed in June, the Mohawks had been amiable and had espoused peace with the French. It might take months, even years, but Jogues was certain the mission would take root and grow into a magnificent gift to God.

Suddenly, a band of Mohawks with faces and bodies streaked with red paint, closed in on Jogues and de la Lande. As they danced and shouted death threats, Jogues stood riveted to the path with de la Lande beside him. Jogues knew that the fragile peace had collapsed.

On the trail back to Ossernenon, the war party, members of the Bear clan, stripped Jogues and de la Lande of their clothes, then kicked and struck them until blood flowed.

When the party reached the palisades of Ossernenon and entered the village, a montage of angry faces and voices assailed Jogues and his companion. "We will kill you," the voices shouted. "You are demons, evildoers!" The anger and hatred of the people moved Jogues to tears.

Then a woman pushed her way to the front of the crowd. Stretching out her arms, she held back the throng of people. It was Jogues' adopted "aunt" and she was not about to let anything happen to him or his young companion. She and her son led Jogues and de la Lande along, shouting at the crowd: Jogues belonged to her! Although the people grumbled and protested, according to Mohawk custom the priest and his companion were allowed to take refuge in the house of his adoption. The code of hospitality was honored, and Jogues and de la Lande would be safe, at least for now.

Something had gone terribly wrong since Jogues' last visit. Jogues soon learned of the disasters that had occurred during his absence. The corn harvests had failed and sickness and famine had plagued the villages. The Huron prisoners, who were unfriendly toward the French, spoke disparagingly of Jogues and the missioners. The Hurons claimed that the blackrobes had always brought disease, famine, and all kinds of evil wherever they went. They charged that the black box Jogues had left in the care of his "aunt" contained an evil spirit, one that would bring disaster to all the Iroquois.

Once again, a Great Council convened to evaluate the peace. The elderly chiefs smoked their calumets as they listened to the arguments of each clan. The Wolf and Turtle clans recalled their promises at Three Rivers. They would remain faithful to their agreement with the French. The Bear clan dissented. They would continue in their hostility against the French and their emissaries, Jogues and de la Lande. The chiefs used all their diplomatic skills to cool the hostile members of the Bear clan, but they remained adamant. Jogues knew that he and de la Lande were in great danger. He prayed to God to soften the hearts of the angry men. The new mission he came to establish in Mohawk country, a mission that could promote peace and unity among the various nations as well as the French, would bring people to Christ.

On October 18, 1646, as Jogues was praying in his cabin, he heard a voice call to him from outside the bark door. "Ondessonk, come. We invite you to a feast." In the waning light of evening, Jogues recognized the young man as a member of the Bear clan. If he declined the invitation, Jogues might jeopardize the peace efforts. He also risked offending his host and giving the impression that he was a coward. He wanted none of these, so he followed the young man to the longhouse where the evening meal was to be served.

Jogues followed him with a prayer on his lips. He sensed danger. When he parted the bark covers of the dwelling, he heard the sound of heavy breathing and without seeing them Jogues knew that there were many men inside. The silence spoke. He immediately knew that his hour had come. Jogues stooped to enter the longhouse and caught the blow of a tomahawk planted deeply into his skull.

Then the dancing and celebrating began! The men rejoiced to have destroyed the great Ondessonk, the blackrobe and French sorcerer! But he would not be the last French victim.

Quiet fell over the longhouse of Jogues' aunt. The disturbance that had interrupted de la Lande's prayer faded. It was growing late. Why had Jogues not returned?

Jogues' aunt sat near the fire and covered her face as she wept. Her voice trembled with anger as she told de la Lande between sobs that Jogues had been murdered. His dear father, Jogues, dead? Overcome with grief, de la Lande stifled his own cry of pain.

De la Lande lay awake on his sleeping shelf, his mind troubled by so many thoughts, his heart heavy with sadness. He decided that he must find Jogues' body. He must retrieve the priest's crucifix and his rosary. He must preserve whatever relics were left and make sure they were sent back to Quebec. He recalled how Jogues had searched René Goupil's body and how nothing had remained.

Quickly, quietly, de la Lande left the safety of the cabin and crept out into the night. Within moments, he heard footsteps. He crouched defenseless in the darkness, his heart beating the heavy rhythm of familiar drums. Suddenly angry cries broke out over him and strong, rough hands dragged him into a moonlit clearing. De la Lande saw for an instant the gleam of a tomahawk. A single blow sank deep into de la Lande's skull and he crumpled to the ground.

The heads of de la Lande and Jogues were placed on a high pole in the palisade for everyone to see. Their bodies were thrown into the river.

CHAPTER TEN

As late as November the French still thought the peace was intact, although Iroquois had been seen hunting in the vicinity as they had in the past. News arrived that some Hurons near Montreal had been captured, and two Frenchmen who had canoed up the St. Lawrence River had vanished. The Jesuits heard nothing from Isaac Jogues and Father Le Jeune, stationed at Montreal for the winter, grew more worried.

Three Rivers, Ville Marie, and Quebec settled into the arms of a mild winter. December passed uneventfully. When spring came, the French expected the Iroquois to travel north. None came. Then reports of houses being ransacked at Three Rivers reached the French. A series of attacks, captures, and massacres followed. The Algonquins were now certain that the Mohawks were on the warpath, and they were eager to pursue them. After much deliberation, Governor Montmagny agreed to send along some French soldiers to strengthen the Algonquin defenses.

Still nothing was heard of Jogues and de la Lande. On June 4, 1647, Otouolti, the Huron friend of the blackrobes, brought news to Three Rivers that Jogues and de la Lande had been killed. Other sources confirmed Otouolti's words. Despite Father Buteux, Father Lalemant, and Governor Montmagny's investigations, the details of the deaths of Jogues and de la Lande remained a mystery. Then two letters arrived for Governor Montmagny from the Dutch colonies, and both attested to the belief that Jogues and de la Lande had been captured and killed by warriors of the Bear Clan. The Dutch believed the Wolf and the Turtle Clans had opposed the action. The correspondence described the torments Jogues and de la Lande had endured, how they had been threatened with death, not by fire, but by the blow of a tomahawk.

During the summer, Iroquois warriors wreaked havoc upon the French colonies and nearby enemy tribes. One day Jean Amyot, the boy Father Jogues had brought to the Hurons ten years earlier and who had grown to manhood, discovered a Mohawk hiding in a hollow tree trunk. The Algonquins promptly claimed him as their prisoner and brought him to Quebec. Father Lalemant wrote of this Mohawk's testimony in the *Relations* for 1646:

Father Jogues, he said, was not killed by the general consent of the Iroquois villages; he was not beaten or stripped, but simply struck down. (I will say in passing, with reference to this matter, that we attach more credence to the letters sent by the Dutch than to the words of this prisoner—because we have strong suspicions that it was he himself who killed the Father.)

This prisoner expressed a desire to learn more about God, and as time went on to know more about the Catholic faith. The priests taught him, answered his questions, and spent hours discerning his motives. They finally agreed that the man had a sincere desire to become a Christian.

On September 15, 1647, Father Druillettes baptized him. Governor Montmagny feared for the well being of this new Christian whom the Hurons were holding in custody. Montmagny ordered the Algonquins to "exact justice from him" only, thus he implied that they were not to torture him.

Although the Mohawk never confessed to killing Jogues, just one year after Father Jogues' death, the Algonquins burned him at the stake and threw his remains into the St. Lawrence River.

In Lalemant's *Relation* for 1647, he wrote of Isaac Jogues:

We have honored this death as the death of a martyr; and although we were in various places, several of our fathers—without knowing aught from one another because of the distances between these places—although they could not resolve to celebrate for him the Mass of the dead, have indeed offered this adorable Sacrifice by way of thanksgiving for the blessings that God had extended to him. The laymen who knew him intimately and the religious houses have honored his death, feeling inclined to invoke the priest rather than to pray for his soul. It is the thought of several learned men and this idea is more than reasonable, that he is truly a martyr before God.... This death is the death of a martyr before the angels.

Indeed, René Goupil, Isaac Jogues, and Jean de la Lande were all regarded as martyrs and saints of the Church. A martyr's blood must not be shed in vain, and the Jesuits were determined to continue the work in their mission field. They worked to instruct the people and convert them to the Faith. The Jesuits' missionary fervor never faltered. The Jesuits advanced their vigorous efforts at Sainte Marie, the center of the Huron missions.

In the winter, Ragueneau, Le Mercier, Chastellain, and Chabanel remained at Sainte Marie, while de Brébeuf traveled to the surrounding villages with Sainte Marie as his base. At Ossossané, Chaumonot had charge of La Conception. Father Antoine Daniel had charge of the villages of Cahiagué to the east and Teanaustayé to the south, while Garnier and Garreau served the Petuns at the Mission of the Apostles. The mosquitoes and other insects were unbearable in the summer; the deep snows and severe cold made it difficult to walk from town to town in the winter. The priests traveled without shelter, sufficient food, and sometimes without welcome from those whom they sought to serve. But these missionaries remained undaunted and hopeful, burning with the desire to bring God's word to all people.

The Iroquois threat rose up anew, but Sainte Marie seemed invincible as a Christian stronghold enclosed within palisades and fortified walls. About 175 feet long and approximately eighty or ninety feet wide, the fort lay 100 feet from the river. The many buildings were constructed of rough wood with chimneys made of local stone. The windows were covered with animal skins to keep out the cold during the winter and the biting insects in the summer. The hospital housed the sick, and the Jesuits and their workmen assisted all those who came to them for help. When famine struck the nearby villages, the priests used their own food supplies to help those in need. By necessity, Sainte Marie had become a citadel; still, the Hurons recognized it as a haven of peace, a dwelling place for God, and a center for Catholic belief and practice.

The following year, Father de Brébeuf, as consultor for the Huron Mission, sent his annual letter to Rome: "From the House of Sainte Marie among the Hurons in New France, June 2, 1648." In the letter de Brébeuf stated:

Under one aspect, the condition of our affairs appears to be most excellent, because at home the utmost peace, union and tranquility flourish among ours and those of our household. All apply themselves most diligently to piety, virtue, and perfection.... Though nothing whatever was brought to us from France in the past year, nevertheless up to this time, we have abundance and superabundance.

De Brébeuf stressed that this prosperity allowed the missioners to extend greater help to the native peoples. De Brébeuf said two obstacles impeded the progress and threatened the mission's existence. "Common to us and all the Hurons," he said, "is the enemy whom we call by the name of Iroquois. On the one hand, they close the roads and obstruct trade; on the other, they devastate this region by frequent massacres. In brief, they fill every place with fear."

The Iroquois' blockade was damaging to New France and the colonists who depended on the Hurons for pelts. In turn, the Hurons needed European goods for trading. Independent French traders also earned their livelihood from the fur trade. Europeans paid high prices to obtain the soft shiny beaver furs, so the market was flourishing.

The other obstacle de Brébeuf spoke about was the hostility some of the non-Christian Hurons nurtured toward the blackrobes. De Brébeuf wrote:

It grew to such a point that a few days ago they killed one of our domestics. They were ready to offer the same treatment to us, if the opportunity had occurred. However, God has turned these latter difficulties into good, and all Hurons have made abundant satisfaction for the death. The Faith, far from receiving any detriment from this, has rather benefited thereby. So true it is that all things work together for the good of those who love God. We trust that it will be the same for all remaining obstacles. For, if God be for us, who is against us?

He expressed admiration for the leadership of Father Paul Ragueneau, judging him an excellent superior of Sainte Marie and her missions. He spoke of his anxiety regarding a successor and believed that when the time came to appoint a new superior, the replacement should be one of the Jesuits at Sainte Marie, not someone from outside the circle of the native environment.

As the time for the annual Spiritual Exercises drew near, Father Antoine Daniel came from Teanaustayé to spend eight days in solitude and prayer. With his soul nourished and his body refreshed, Daniel ended his days of prayer by joining the other missioners in a meal of thanksgiving and celebration. The entire team was once again together, under one roof, and this brought great happiness to each of the priests.

Daniel and de Brébeuf, the two oldest members of the missioners, reminisced about the earlier days. They had both finally mastered the Huron language, which had earned them the esteem of the natives. They had shared many experiences, and now they were sharing memories in the tranquility of the large community room at Sainte Marie. Daniel, now forty-eight years old, was still energetic and enthusiastic though the toil and fatigue of past years was beginning to show. Many nights he had gone without sleep and many days he had gone without food. As de Brébeuf studied his friend, he realized how much Daniel had aged. In spite of de Brébeuf's urging that Daniel stay a few more days to rest, he left Sainte Marie on July 2, 1648, anxious to return to the mission of St. Joseph at Teanaustayé. He left as he had come, wearing his black robe and wide-brimmed hat that the Hurons jokingly described as an upside-down kettle. Daniel carried only his prayer book as he walked with quick steps in the direction of Teanaustayé—a bent figure hurrying toward his home away from home. Devoted to his Christian Hurons, Daniel worked tirelessly to minister to them and to the non-Christians. He never thought of himself, rather, he always thought of others. De Brébeuf felt a sense of foreboding as he watched Daniel leave the protection of the palisades and mount the crest of the small hill that eventually took him from sight.

Daniel arrived at St. Joseph. The next morning he heard birds singing as they fluttered among the leafy branches of oaks, elms, maples, and needled pines. Father Daniel smiled as he prepared for Mass. How he loved the forests in the Huron wilderness. His calloused, work-worn hands set the white altar cloth in place. It had just recently arrived from Montreal, where the sisters at the Hôtel Dieu had embroidered it. As the candles flickered, the sweet scent of beeswax mingled with the perfume of delicate blue wildflowers that Bernadette and Anita, two Huron Christians, had prepared to decorate the altar at the mission of St. Joseph. With the familiar scents came a flood of memories that brought Daniel back to Dieppe, his birthplace. He recalled that happy morning when as a young priest, feeling both humbled and privileged, he had offered his first Mass.

Father Daniel vested for Mass early on July 4, and since the new day was already very warm, he drew back the skins from the windows. He rang the bell, actually an inverted iron kettle, to summon the faithful. The loud clanging echoed throughout the valley, much like the bells he had heard in the small village churches in France.

An ominous-like silence hung in the air. Feeling restless, some of the young men had gone hunting or fishing. Others had gone in search of Iroquois who had been sighted in the area. Women and children, the elderly and infirm, remained unprotected in the village.

Daniel smiled in welcome through his thick black beard, his expressive eyes lighting with pleasure as, one by one, the faithful filed into the small chapel. Renewed in spirit from his recent retreat, he preached a vigorous homily encouraging the faithful Christians to hold fast to their belief in God. He counseled them against falling back into some of their old ways, and spoke of the promise of life everlasting that awaited them. Father Daniel raised his hand in blessing at the conclusion of Mass and the small congregation prepared to leave. Suddenly, a cry of terror shattered the early morning calm. "Ho-de-no-sau-nee! Ho-de-no-sau-nee! The enemy! The enemy has come!"

A wave of fear for the safety of his flock came over Daniel. He watched the panic rising on the people's faces as they rushed to him and begged the priest to save them. Some asked to be baptized; he administer the sacrament by taking a large white handkerchief, dipping it into the fount, and baptized by aspersion. He also pronounced the words of absolution and then pleaded with his people to run, to escape. Instead, they began pulling him toward the door. He must escape with them. Daniel, however, insisted that the people flee the stockade while they still had time. He would remain. The war had begun and the fallen Hurons would need him. The wounded Iroquois would also need help; perhaps some would even ask for baptism.

As the war cries of the Iroquois crescendoed through the settlement, Daniel drew himself up to his full height and strode resolutely toward the chapel doors, ready to face the Iroquois. His only thought was of saving the people of Teanaustayé. He raised a crucifix aloft and advanced fearlessly toward the enemy, to meet them where they stood. At the sight of the priest dressed in his red vestments, the warriors hesitated. Who was this man who showed no fear? What powers did he have? Did he think he could destroy them? Outraged, they resumed their attack. Arrows and a volley of gunshot brought Daniel down. His was stripped, scalped, and laid to waste by those who wanted to consume his courage. Some of the warriors milled around, chanting their victory cry until they set fire to the chapel and tossed the priest's body into the raging inferno that consumed him. Thus did Antoine Daniel die, and with him hundreds of Huron men, women, and children in the village of Teanaustayé. The Iroquois had killed or captured more than 700 Hurons that day. But because of Daniel's selfless courage far more had been able to escape in the direction of Sainte Marie. A company of Iroquois stayed behind to claim the spoils; then they trotted along the trail toward their encampment while singing songs of triumph.

The priests at Sainte Marie became alarmed when they caught sight of the cloud of black smoke rising up from the direction of Teanaustayé, bringing with it the stench of charred wood and death. Within hours, the Hurons who had escaped confirmed what the priests at Sainte Marie had feared. Paul Ragueneau and everyone at the mission received the news of the destruction of St. Joseph's with great sorrow. The Jesuit's immediately sent runners to alert the priests at all the missions. The Iroquois were surely on their way to destroy more of the Huron villages—no one was safe. Numbed by the news of Daniel's death, de Brébeuf decided to travel to Teanaustayé to see the devastation for himself. Perhaps he would find some article of Daniel's—a rosary or crucifix. De Brébeuf remembered Jogues describing his search for Goupil's body. He felt compelled to investigate the scene and to salvage whatever he could find that had belonged to this latest martyr.

De Brébeuf approached the ruins of the village with a heavy heart. Smoke still rose from the charred ruins of the buildings. He grieved for the dead Hurons, whose bodies were strewn along every path. De Brébeuf made his way to the burned chapel and began sifting through the ashes. His heart ached for the stricken Hurons and for Daniel, his friend and gifted missionary. He was certain that the missions had another powerful intercessor in heaven. Goupil, de la Lande, Jogues, and now Daniel, all martyrs, all saints. In the deep silence of the deserted village, de Brébeuf prayed that he might face his death with the same courage. He returned to Sainte Marie with the news of what he had seen.

A cloud seemed to hang over the mission as the year moved into a harsh winter. Spring took a long time to appear and the March winds blew as cold as winter, though some of the smaller streams had begun to thaw. The priests who staffed the missions came together for their annual conferences at Sainte Marie and to review the fruits of the year's labors.

After discussions and prayers, they assembled at a long table to share their evening meal. Father Chaumonot took his place facing a white wall. The candlelight cast shadows on the wall, and as the candle flame flickered and danced, so did the shadows. Suddenly Father Chaumonot stood up, staring wide-eyed at a spot in front of him. "Father Antoine!" he exclaimed. "Father Antoine is here!" The priests looked questioningly at one another. They could see nothing. Ragueneau later wrote, "We felt his presence strengthening us with his courage, filling us with his light and the spirit of God that invested him." No one there felt Daniel's presence more strongly than Father de Brébeuf. He would soon be called to summon all the courage he had.

CHAPTER ELEVEN

Eight months had passed since the destruction of St. Joseph's mission, but the memory of the disaster lingered in de Brébeuf's mind and heart. Already fifty-five years old, de Brébeuf still worked with as much vigor as he had in his younger days. Although his travels on foot or by canoe were becoming more difficult, his missionary fervor never diminished. His devotion to Jesus, to the Blessed Mother, and to St. Joseph deepened as time went on. Now he and Father Gabriel Lalemant were working at the mission of St. Louis.

De Brébeuf added more kindling to the hearth fire and lit another lamp in the dark and drafty room. A March storm had loosened some shingles covering the longhouse and the roof needed immediate repair. He and Lalemant had decided to work together to mend the damage after Mass before traveling to St. Ignace, a short distance from St. Louis. They planned to arrive there in the afternoon, and would celebrate Mass with the Christian Hurons the following morning.

Gabriel Lalemant was the nephew of two other priests: Charles Lalemant, the Jesuit pioneer of early Quebec, and Jerome Lalemant, the former superior of the Huron missions. Gabriel's oldest brother was a Carthusian monk and all three of his sisters had entered convents. When Gabriel made his first profession as a Jesuit in 1632, he also made a private vow to dedicate himself to the foreign missions. However, it was not until September of 1646 that Lalemant arrived in New France. Two years later, he finally made it to Huronia. Gabriel Lalemant, whom the villagers called Atironta, joined de Brébeuf in the mission. Looking younger than his thirty-eight years, he was slight in stature and of frail health, but he burned with a zeal that de Brébeuf admired. His yearning was to preach the Gospel to the native peoples and he worked tirelessly at de Brébeuf's side, tending to the needs at the missions of St. Louis, St. Anne, and four other small villages, as well as St. Ignace, the newest village. The two priests traveled from village to village through deep snow, in freezing rain and bitter cold. Gabriel Lalemant had prayed daily to be sent to the Hurons and, that prayer answered, he had a strong desire to be found worthy to shed his blood for Jesus Christ.

De Brébeuf looked at the gray sky. Winter was nearly over, but most of the Hurons stayed in their old longhouses. Last autumn, de Brébeuf had feared for their safety because somewhere in the area the Iroquois were hiding, waiting. How many? When would they strike? No one knew. He had urged the people of St. Louis to move to a new site, a strip of level land surrounded on three sides by ravines forty feet deep. The chiefs had heeded de Brébeuf's suggestion to build triple stockades as fortifications that would make the town impenetrable. The nearby stream made it an ideal location. The Hurons had been enthusiastic and, at first, the work progressed. But their enthusiasm dwindled. It seemed that the destruction of St. Joseph's mission had sown seeds of doom in the hearts of the Huron people. They had grown apathetic and merely awaited what they believed to be their inevitable fate.

After Mass, the two priests climbed to the roof to repair the storm's damage. Lalemant held the sheets of bark while de Brébeuf secured them. The work did not take long, but by the time they finished, de Brébeuf's fingers were numb. As they turned to enter their longhouse, they caught sight of three Hurons, naked and running, coming from the direction of St. Ignace. As the runners drew closer, their shouts raised the dreaded alarm: "The Iroquois! The Ho-de-no-sau-nee! They have entered the new village. Soon they will be here!"

Cries of panic swept through the village. What they had feared most during the long winter months was about to happen. The enemy was upon them. The village would be destroyed and they would all die. De Brébeuf and Lalemant tried to calm the people as they hurried from house to house, helping the women to gather whatever food and clothing they could carry. They tried to soothe the terrified children and helped the elders in their feeble efforts to escape. The priests baptized those who asked and gave absolution to the Christians. They encouraged the people to pray and urged them to escape while there was time.

Stephen Annaotaha assembled a small number of warriors who would defend St. Louis. "Echon! Atironta!" Stephen shouted. "You must go while there is still time. Save yourselves!" De Brébeuf shook his head; he would remain. He belonged with the warriors who would either perish in the battle or be taken prisoner. He urged Lalemant to leave and hurry back to Sainte Marie, but the younger priest was determined to remain with de Brébeuf.

De Brébeuf watched the fleeing Hurons disappear into the thick forest, and he prayed for their safety. "Some will make it to Sainte Marie," he thought aloud, "and others will hide in the woods only to be captured." Abruptly, de Brébeuf shook himself out of his thoughts and turned to run toward the stockaded walls. Time was running out.

An eerie stillness hung over the village. Weapons in hand, the Huron warriors waited alert and ready to attack. But de Brébeuf knew they could not match the enemy. The flimsy defense could not hold out against the Iroquois for long.

Suddenly shrill war cries pierced the silence as the Iroquois burst from the surrounding forest. De Brébeuf made the sign of the cross. The time had come! The sound of musket fire mingled with the cries of wounded men while arrows flew and landed everywhere. De Brébeuf and Lalemant moved from one wounded or dead Huron to the next, baptizing, absolving, praying. All the while, more Iroquois poured in from the forest. They hacked at the palisades and chopped through the barrier and ran into the village, quickly overpowering Annaotaha and his men. De Brébeuf watched in a sorrow mingled with admiration as the sixty Hurons who had fought so bravely dropped their weapons and courageously surrendered to the enemy.

The Iroquois conquerors had smeared themselves with the warm blood of the victims of St. Ignace which, mixed with the red war paint. Victory cries rang out as the Iroquois tied the wrists of their captives. The prisoners were commanded to sing as they were jostled and pushed along the path to St. Ignace, while the black smoke billowed up to the clouds from St. Louis.

As they moved along, the captives were stripped and beaten. Yet, de Brébeuf raised his voice in praise of God and urged the Hurons to do likewise. Lalemant, thin, pale, and shivering in the cold wind, raised his voice with the others. De Brébeuf knew that soon they would all suffer unspeakable tortures. He had prayed for the gift of martyrdom and so had Lalemant. They were ready. But what of Annaotaha and the Christian Hurons?

The Iroquois forced the prisoners to form two lines and made them run the gauntlet, taunting, beating, and scourging them. When the torturers paused, de Brébeuf told Lalemant that they would soon be put to death. Should Lalemant survive the ordeal, de Brébeuf urged him to escape. They spoke their final farewells and then absolved one another.

Thick gray clouds eclipsed the noon sun as the priests and the Hurons were led to a great longhouse, the one de Brébeuf had planned to use as the chapel for the new village. In the cabin, the torture posts stood visible and ready.

De Brébeuf was the first. He was commanded to dance and sing his death song. He complied and sang his prayers while two Iroquois beat him with sticks as they mocked the mighty Echon who was now in their power. The bones in his hands had been broken, his fingers severed. Then, bound to the post, he was tortured with clubs and spears that were supposed to wring cries for mercy from de Brébeuf. He suffered excruciating pain but he summoned all his strength, a strength that was rooted in the Lord, and he never uttered so much as a groan.

The torture continued: boiling water was poured over his head and shoulders in derision of baptism; hot hatchets were applied to the most sensitive parts of his body; a collar of red-hot hatchets was placed around his neck; a "belt" made of bark filled with pitch and resin was placed around his waist and then set afire. De Brébeuf "seemed insensible to fire and flame, never uttered a cry, and remained so perfectly silent that he astonished even his torturers" (*Jesuit Relations*).

Then, as if regaining his senses, he encouraged the other captives to pray, "*Jesus, taiteur!*" (Jesus, have mercy.) Again and again he cried out, "*Jesus, taiteur!*" Again and again Lalemant and the Christian Hurons echoed the prayer. This enraged his torturers. They were determined to silence the great blackrobe, so they cut out his tongue, mutilated his face, then tore away the covering of his skull.

De Brébeuf reached the height of his agony at about three o'clock on the same day he was captured. Before he died, his heart was torn out and consumed by those who wanted a portion of Echon's courage.

On Tuesday, March 16, about four in the afternoon, Jean de Brébeuf entered the glory of the martyrs. He was only nine days short of his fifty-ninth birthday. His life ended as he had desired—in Huron country, among those whom he had ministered to with untiring zeal.

Meanwhile, tied to a stake, Lalemant witnessed his mentor's agony and death while knowing his own would soon follow. Could worse tortures than those meted out to de Brébeuf be devised? Lalemant received strength from de Brébeuf's example. But what of the Hurons? Who would encourage them, comfort them, pray with them? Lalemant seemed to feel the spirit of de Brébeuf giving him the strength and courage to face the suffering to come.

Lalemant was brought to his feet and roused to full consciousness. Like the other captives, he had been repeatedly burned and beaten and could hardly stand. Still he prayed aloud, *"Jesus taiteur."* The Hurons followed his lead.

Angered by his constant murmuring and believing that Lalemant was cursing the Iroquois Nation, a young man struck the priest a terrible blow. "Stop!" a comrade called out. "He cannot die tonight. He will be sacrificed in the morning to Areskoui, the god of sun, the god of war. Feed him so that he will live until the sun rises."

As morning light filtered through the smoke hole of the longhouse, Lalemant was dragged outside to suffer the same tortures de Brébeuf had endured: boiling water, the red hot necklace of glowing hatchets, the belt of pitch and bark, and as he prayed, the severing of his tongue and burning coals fixed to his eyes. Lalemant endured his torture from six o'clock Tuesday evening until nine o'clock the next morning, March 17, when the blow of a tomahawk ended his suffering.

On the day of the attack one of the *engagés* at work on a rooftop at Sainte Marie caught sight of smoke rising above the forest. He hurried to inform Father Ragueneau. By the time they climbed the barricade, the smoke was already billowing up into the clouds. Ragueneau estimated the distance and realized the fire was coming from St. Louis. He hurried back to the house with sorrow in his heart and a prayer on his lips for Lalemant and de Brébeuf. They had planned to leave for St. Ignace; perhaps they had left in time.

Ragueneau sent several *donnés* to hurry the three miles to St. Louis, but no sooner had they left the safety of Sainte Marie than a party of Huron warriors broke out of the forest, running toward the mission. The warriors had escaped from St. Ignace and had seen the two priests at St. Louis, and now, they warned, the Iroquois would come to destroy Sainte Marie.

Small groups of women and children carrying all they owned sought refuge at Sainte Marie. One by one, battle-weary and wounded Huron warriors arrived, bringing the news that Echon and Atironta had been captured. Although he had hoped otherwise, Ragueneau was certain they had been tortured and killed.

He was equally certain that Sainte Marie was in great danger. The *donnés*, *engages*, and the few soldiers assembled, armed with muskets and whatever defense weapons they could find. A handful of Hurons joined the guard. Ragueneau feared for the women and children still hiding in the forest. If the Iroquois attacked they would be massacred, but the area within the stockade was already filled to capacity. Still, the Huron refugees continued to arrive, cold, hungry, and weary from the long walk in the snow. The Jesuits shared their food and provided warmth and shelter to all who came.

The attack could come at any time. The pink sunset faded into gray. The Iroquois had not arrived, and the defense slept with muskets in hand. The priests filed into the chapel to pray. In the morning, 300 Hurons passed by Sainte Marie and disappeared into the forest as they headed for St. Louis. Ragueneau learned later that the Hurons met a large band of Iroquois and vicious fighting ensued. The Hurons faced their enemies in hand-to-hand combat, and though for a time they seemed to be winning the battle, they could not keep their advantage. A large band of Iroquois on their way to Sainte Marie joined the battle. The badly outnumbered Hurons fell back, and only about twenty Christian Hurons survived. When they returned to Sainte Marie, Ragueneau learned what had happened. He mourned the fate of the Huron converts and of the entire Huron Nation. The news that about 1,200 Iroquois were headed for Sainte Marie to destroy the mission made his very soul cry out to God to spare the remaining priests. They prayed to their patron, St. Joseph, and promised to offer a Mass in his honor every month for the coming year. On March 18, the eve of St. Joseph's feast, the priests celebrated the first Mass and then waited. Silence fell over the forest. Where were the Iroquois?

CHAPTER TWELVE

The Hurons and Jesuits at Sainte Marie kept their uneasy vigil. But, as Ragueneau later wrote, on the feast of St. Joseph a sudden and inexplicable terror fell upon the Iroquois and they retreated in fear. For the time being, Sainte Marie had been spared. The priests believed that the mission had been protected from harm through St. Joseph's intercession.

Stephen Annaotaha, the chief who had witnessed the attack on St. Louis, arrived at the mission and related details of the deaths of Echon and Atironta. He told of his own escape and how he had pleaded with the priests to escape as well, but they chose to remain with their people.

The Jesuits at Sainte Marie felt a deep sadness when they learned how their brothers de Brébeuf and Lalemant had sacrificed their lives. Appalled by the circumstances of their deaths, Ragueneau sent Jacques Bonin, Regnault, Malherb, and several other *donnés* to recover the bodies of these latest martyrs.

Stephen and the others traveled the six miles to St. Ignace and wept at what they saw there. In the smoking ruins lay hundreds of Hurons, their dead bodies strewn among those of the Iroquois. Stephen led the men to the spot where de Brébeuf had endured his final tortures. Here his burned and blackened body lay near Lalemant's. Father Bonnin and the *donnés* placed the remains on a stretcher, and in reverent silence, the small band made their way back to Sainte Marie.

Silence fell over the mission as the men returned with the bodies of the martyrs. The priests gathered to pray and to mourn the loss of their holy and courageous confreres. Regnault testified:

> They were brought to our cabin and laid uncovered upon the bark of trees. I examined them there at leisure for more than two hours to see if what the Indians had told us of their martyrdom and death was true. I examined first the body of Father de Brébeuf, which was pitiful to see, as well as that of Father Lalemant. Father de Brébeuf had his legs, thighs and arms stripped of flesh to the very bone. I saw and touched a large number of great blisters, which he had on several places on his body, from the boiling water, which had been poured over him in mockery of holy Baptism. I saw and touched the wounds from a belt of bark full of pitch and resin, which roasted his whole body. I saw and touched the marks of burns from the collars of hatchets placed on his shoulders and stomach. I saw and touched his two lips, which they had cut off because he constantly spoke of God while they made him suffer. I saw and touched all parts of his body, which had received more than 200 blows from cudgels. I saw and touched the top of the scalped head. I saw and touched the opening, which had been made to tear out his heart. In fine, I saw and touched all the wounds of his body, as the Indians had told and declared to us.

> We buried these precious relics on Sunday, March 21, with so much consolation and so much tender devotion in all who were present at the obsequies, that I know none who did not desire, rather than fear, a similar death, and who did not regard himself as blessed to live in a place where, perhaps a few days from thence God would accord him the grace of shedding on a similar occasion both his blood and his life.

None of the priests could bring themselves to pray for de Brébeuf or Lalemant, for they believed there was no need—the souls of their beloved friends were in heaven interceding for them.

When Father Ragueneau recovered the personal writings of the two martyrs, he found these words written by Lalemant, "Let us then, O my soul, in a spirit of piety, lose ourselves entirely to bring consolation to the Sacred Heart of Jesus Christ; he deserves it and it is a strict duty for us to give it to him, unless we wish to live and die spurning his love." Before his arrival in New France, Lalemant had expressed his desire to die for the glory of God—for martyrdom. He was the last to join the Jesuit missionaries in Huronia, but among the first to have his desire fulfilled.

De Brébeuf's spiritual notes contained thoughts he had often shared with Ragueneau. He vowed to serve God ever more perfectly and wrote of his burning desire to suffer more for Christ.

"My Lord Jesus, if the grace of martyrdom is ever mercifully offered by you to me, your unworthy servant, I shall not fail to accept this grace. Grant that I may so live that you will accord me the grace to die for you. Thus, my Lord, I shall accept your chalice and I shall call upon your name: Jesus, Jesus, Jesus.... I trust that God will always help me. Aided by his grace, I do not fear the terrible torments of fire any more than I fear the prick of a pin."

Ragueneau felt the tears welling up in his eyes as he read de Brébeuf's words of love and dedication to God. He had been the first apostle to the Hurons, had administered thousands of baptisms, and had preached the Gospel message to people who had never known Christianity. De Brébeuf had been the most loved of all the missionaries with his hearty laughter, his good humor, his humility, his love for everyone.

"It appeared," wrote Father Bressani, "that God had determined to put an end to the mission of the Hurons at the same time that he put an end to the life of him who had begun it. This was Father Jean de Brébeuf. At his death, the irreparable ruin of the Huron Nation began."

Within a short time after de Brébeuf's death, fifteen Huron villages were abandoned. When new leaves appeared on the bare trees in the spring, few Hurons were there to welcome the season. The worn paths that connected the scattered towns no longer felt the running strides of moccasined feet. The rivers no longer carried Huron canoes, and the soft breezes mourned the absence of Huron voices. Hundreds of Hurons still camped throughout the countryside surrounding Sainte Marie, while the priests wondered how they could minister to a people now so widely scattered. Often Ragueneau lay awake at night planning how best to meet the Hurons' spiritual needs. Food from the mission storehouses was shared with the survivors around Sainte Marie, but with many Hurons still in hiding, many went hungry as famine gripped the land again. Almost the entire Bear Nation of the Hurons fled to the land of the Petuns. Others sought protection among the Neutrals and the Eries. The Algonquins took in many Hurons, and some refugees found safety on nearby islands.

The knowledge that the Iroquois would indeed come plagued Ragueneau; they would certainly raid Sainte Marie. He had to do something, but what? He had to find a way to continue the mission. They could not abandon the Hurons. The only possible solution seemed to Ragueneau to be the construction of a new Sainte Marie far enough away to escape the Iroquois. The priests discussed the matter. They had to move as quickly as possible, and the most logical site was the island of Ekaentoton, situated 180 miles north, which had already been named Sainte Marie. Many Hurons were already building homes there and forming a village. The route to Quebec was open from there.

The priests attended a council with twelve Huron chiefs who spoke with characteristic eloquence and persuasion. Ragueneau and his missioners listened to the words of the Huron leaders who had decided to move to Ekaentoton, but now changed their minds. Their reasoning persuaded the missionaries who agreed that the island of Ahoendoe would be a better location for the new mission. This settlement, which the missioners had already named St. Joseph, would unite the Hurons, and perhaps in a few years they would find a way to return to the mainland.

Ragueneau later wrote, "We could not doubt that God had chosen to speak to us by their lips. Although at their [the Huron chiefs'] coming we had decided upon another plan, we all found ourselves changed before their departure. With unanimous consent, we believed that it was necessary to follow God in the direction wither he chose to call us...for the remaining future...whatever peril there may be in it for us, in whatever depth of darkness we may continue in."

Once the decision was made, the priests lost no time in preparing to move. The carpenters built a small but sturdy barge and a roughly crafted raft. The priests, the *donnés*, the *engages*, and all the workmen packed up the food supplies that would be needed in the coming winter months, as well as clothing, snowshoes, and boots. They packed with special care the sacred vessels for Mass, as well as their precious books and writings. Although they would have liked to take along other items, the barge and raft could not hold the weight. They would burn what they had to leave behind.

They treasured the bones of de Brébeuf and Lalemant as their most precious possession. These above all else had to be preserved. Molere and Regnault unearthed the bodies of the two martyrs and boiled them in strong lye, then placed the bones in a small clay oven to dry and harden them. Father Ragueneau wrapped the relics in silk cloth and placed them in two small chests. Later, these were brought to Quebec.

They had finished their preparations by early summer and on Monday, June 14, they loaded the barge and raft. The Jesuit missionaries prayed their farewells at the altar of their beloved house at Sainte Marie; then Ragueneau gave orders and the *donnés* set fire to the chapel, the buildings, the stockades, and the cabins outside the palisades. The priests and workmen rushed to the barge and paddled away as quickly as possible. Sainte Marie, the mission that had seen ten years of dedicated labor and self-sacrifice, went up in flames.

In the *Relations*, Father Ragueneau described their departure:

We have left our dwelling place, rather I might call it our delight…. We even applied the torch to the work of our own hands, lest the sacred house should furnish shelter to the enemy. In a single day and almost in a moment, we saw consumed our work of nearly ten years.

It was between five and six o'clock in the evening that part of our number embarked in a small vessel that we had built. I, in company with most of the others, trusted myself to a sort of raft that should float on that faithless element. We voyaged all night upon our great lake by dint of arms and oars; and we landed without mishap, after a few days, upon an island where the Hurons were awaiting us…that we might make of it a Christian Island…the Island of St. Joseph.

The French set out immediately to construct the buildings needed for the mission at Ahoendoe, felling trees from the nearby forest and clearing the land. Priests, *donnés* and *engagés* worked tirelessly side by side to finish before winter. Every day more Hurons, mostly women, children, and the elderly, came and began to build their own longhouses at Ahoendoe. The population swelled to 1,000 by autumn, and most of the people had been without sufficient food since March. Ragueneau recognized the plight of the Christian Hurons and he suffered with them. There was little food even for his own priests and workmen, yet he did not turn anyone away hungry. Ragueneau worried over their desperate situation and spent hours in prayer during the night. Then, as if sent by God, a group of Algonquin missioners brought 600 bushels of acorns and an abundance of dried fish. Although Ragueneau was indeed grateful, he knew this was not enough to save the Hurons.

The first snow fell in November, softly at first, then furiously. The lake froze and the Iroquois lurked on the mainland. Food was scarcer than ever before. Pneumonia and influenza entered the longhouses, and one by one, those weakened from hunger died. Ragueneau anguished over the situation, knowing that his beloved Hurons would not survive. Then, on a cold, windy day, two Christian Hurons who had escaped from the Iroquois made their way to the mission with alarming news.

CHAPTER THIRTEEN

The runners said that the Iroquois had attacked Petun villages, promising to return to burn and destroy those that remained. Ragueneau was concerned for Fathers Charles Garnier and Noël Chabanel, who were in charge of the Petun village of Etarita. Adrien Grélon and Leonard Garreau were presently in the outlying hills. Ragueneau sent word immediately to all the priests, recalling them immediately to Sainte Marie II unless there was an exceptional reason to remain among the Petuns. Garnier reasoned that, in spite of the danger from the Iroquois, the Petuns at Etarita should not be abandoned.

A priest was greatly needed at Etarita, but one would be enough, so Garnier sent Chabanel back to Sainte Marie II. Garnier had recently written to Ragueneau, "I have no fears about my health. What I should fear more would be that of deserting my flock in their misery of hunger and amidst the terrors of war, since they need me more than ever. I would fail to use the opportunity that God gives me of losing myself for him and thereafter be unworthy of his favors.... At all times, I am ready to leave everything, even to die in the spirit of obedience. I shall never come down from the cross on which his goodness has placed me."

Reluctantly, Chabanel left Garnier. "I'll go," he said, "where my obedience calls me. Whether or not I shall obtain from my superior the favor of returning to the mission, I do not know. But God must be served till death." Chabanel was accompanied by a group of Christian Hurons who decided it was wise to depart for Ahoendoe rather than await the Iroquois' fury. On December 5, 1649, after Sunday Mass, Chabanel began the trip back to Sainte Marie.

At the mission, Garnier evangelized both the Hurons and the Petuns who had been attracted to Christianity and who now loved and admired the priest. They saw him making the rounds every day in Etarita, visiting the cabins, ministering to the sick, and preaching the word of God. On Tuesday, December 7, Garnier was completing his daily visit to the cabins when he heard the cry: "The Iroquois! The Iroquois!"

Garnier rushed outside, only to see the Iroquois pouring through the gates of the village, their faces painted, their voices raised in the war cry. They cut down young and old, men, women and children. Garnier raced to the chapel where he told the people to escape, to run while they could, and to cherish their faith until death. "Ouracha, save yourself. Come with us!" they pleaded. But Garnier refused. He would remain to baptize and to absolve.

Garnier met his death while performing this ministry. While running from one blazing cabin to another, he felt the searing pain of a bullet in his chest and then another in his lower abdomen. He fell to the ground with the name of Jesus on his lips.

When Garnier regained consciousness a short time later, he had already been stripped of his cassock; blood flowed from his wounds, reddening the snow in which he lay. He saw that only a few yards away a Petun warrior had received a mortal blow, but was still alive. Garnier rose to his knees, stood up, and tried to move toward the dying man only to fall to the ground. He again got to his feet with great effort, took a few steps, and fell. A third time he tried to rise and move closer to the warrior, but he had lost too much blood. A woman hiding nearby witnessed the scene and reported it afterward. Sometime later, an Iroquois warrior struck Garnier on each temple. His body was then completely stripped and left to lie in the snow.

Some of the Hurons fled to Ekarenniondi where Grélon and Garreau resided. When the priests heard news of the attack, they traveled to Etarita as soon as it was safe. As they approached the smoldering ruins of the village, the smell of charred flesh and burned bark nauseated them. A dense cloud of smoke hung over the village and the dead lay everywhere. The priests saw the bodies of the Iroquois, the Petuns, and some Hurons, but they could not find the remains of Garnier. When they came across the charred remains of a body covered with blood and ashes from the fire that had swept over it, the Christian villagers recognized it as Garnier's—their pastor who had died for love of them. Grélon and Garreau cleansed the body as best they could, wrapped it in some of their own clothing, and buried it in the same spot where the church had been. The *Relations* states: "The poverty of the burial was great and the sacredness no less."

Meanwhile, Father Noël Chabanel and the small band of Huron Christians continued their journey to Sainte Marie II, unaware of the attack on Garnier's mission. On the morning of December 7, after having spent the night at the mission of St. Matthias, Chabanel said his farewells to the two priests stationed there. Only thirty-six years old, he had been in the Huron missions since 1643. For him, being a missionary was a living martyrdom. He found it difficult to adjust to the living conditions and after six years had not been able to grasp the Huron language. He had been a professor of rhetoric in France, and he felt humiliated by his inability. Everything about the missions weighed on him: the food that he could never get used to, the climate, the lack of privacy, and the unfamiliar customs of the native people.

He felt continually tempted to give up and return to France. A deep spiritual darkness fell upon him, yet he made a vow to serve God in the Huron missions until death. Chabanel had been stationed at the mission of St. Louis before Gabriel Lalemant replaced him there. Only one month later, Lalemant suffered martyrdom, and Chabanel felt that this showed he was not worthy of martyrdom. He wrote in a letter to his brother in France, who was also a Jesuit, "Your Reverence missed, by a very narrow margin, having a brother a martyr. But before God one must have virtue of a different kind than mine before meriting the honor of martyrdom."

Now he had escaped martyrdom yet again. The band journeyed throughout the day, traveling about eighteen miles over rough terrain. By nightfall they were still in the forest, so his companions set up camp and went to sleep. Chabanel remained awake to pray.

He heard loud noises coming from the road just beyond their camp. Shouts of victory and Iroquois war songs mixed with the cries of the prisoners that had been taken that day at the village of St. John. Chabanel awakened his companions, who immediately disappeared into the woods only to regroup farther down the road where the enemy had just passed.

Father Chabanel tried to follow from a distance, but could not keep up. Finally, he collapsed from exhaustion. He urged the others to go on without him. "What difference does it make if I die or not? This life does not count for much. The Iroquois cannot snatch the happiness of heaven from me."

It is believed that Chabanel changed course at daybreak and began making his way toward Sainte Marie II. A Huron, a former Christian, later reported that as he passed along on the river, he saw the priest standing on the opposite bank. He saw the missionary toss aside his coat, his blanket, and the sack he was carrying before attempting to cross the river, probably to escape more quickly. From that day, December 8, the Feast of the Immaculate Conception, nothing more was ever heard of Father Noël Chabanel.

In the *Relations*, Ragueneau reported that the Jesuits could not be entirely certain how Chabanel died. Possibly, he was captured by the Iroquois who had actually killed some thirty people along the same road that Chabanel would have been traveling. Perhaps he lost his way in the woods and died of fatigue, hunger, and cold. The Jesuits thought it most probable, however, that he had been killed by the Huron who was the last to see him. Although the Huron had told a convincing story about how he had helped the missionary cross the water, later that same Huron was heard boasting that he had killed the blackrobe, stolen his belongings, and thrown his body into the water.

Garnier. Chabanel. The martyrs now totaled eight.

The New Year, 1650, came and the Hurons and the French were still imprisoned on the Island of St. Joseph. They lived in constant fear of the Iroquois. Ragueneau wrote, "Our sleep was but half-sleep. Whatever the cold, whatever the snow, whatever winds might blow, sentinels kept watch all night long, exposed to every severity of weather in the never-ending rounds. The others who, during this time, were taking their period of sleep, were always under arms, as if awaiting the signal for battle."

Deep snow covered the land, burying the acorns and hiding the edible roots, while the Iroquois prevented the Hurons from hunting for game. Famine squeezed life out of the Hurons and brought its danger to Ragueneau's door. The missioners' supply of corn would not last until spring. "Scarcely anyone who is alive," wrote Ragueneau, "does not live by our aid. Hardly any who have died have not acknowledged that they owed more to our charity than to even their own relatives."

The priests buried the bodies of those whom the Hurons could not. Somehow, they managed to survive the winter, albeit gaunt and undernourished, while the dwindling population of Hurons continued to suffer from starvation, disease, and the ever-present threat of Iroquois attack. In April, a band of Hurons ventured out to fish, but they were massacred by the Iroquois. Ragueneau's fear for the mission escalated.

When word arrived that two large Iroquois war parties were planning an attack on Sainte Marie II at Ahoendoe Island, Ragueneau and the Christian Hurons offered prayers to St. Joseph and all the saints. The fate of the Jesuit mission in Huronia was at stake. Relentlessly, the Iroquois were accomplishing their ambition to destroy the Huron people and drive out the French from the territory they intended to dominate. The priests discussed the situation day after day, trying to decide a course of action that would benefit the Hurons as well as the missionary efforts of the Jesuits. Then two of the elder chiefs came to Ragueneau with a plea. "Cast your eyes toward Quebec.... Do not wait until famine and war have violently killed the last one of us. Bear us in your hands and in your heart." Ragueneau spent long hours in the chapel praying for guidance. Should they move the mission a third time and go to Ekaentoton? Would it be cowardly to return to the St. Lawrence, abandoning the missions in Huronia?

The land was awakening to spring, as trees began to bud and the lake and streams thawed. Fish swam to the waters' surface. Bears emerged from their winter lairs, and the cycle of life continued. The new life all around him contrasted with the shadow that fell over Ragueneau's heart. Sickness, famine, and an all-consuming fear of the Iroquois were the constant companions of the Hurons.

Paul Ragueneau recounted the situation of the Huron Nation in these words: "We...became more and more convinced that God was talking to us through the mouthpiece of these captains, because we saw that what they said was only too true; the Huron country was now nothing but a land of horror, devastated by massacres. No matter where we looked, we knew that famine on the one hand and war on the other would finally exterminate the few remaining Christians." After much prayer and consultation among the priests, they decided to abandon the mission. They would give hospitality to any of the Hurons who wished to go with them and settle in Montreal, Three Rivers, or Quebec. Approximately 300 Hurons decided to accompany the priests on the journey. A few were determined to remain, but held no resentment toward those who wished to leave. Once again, the priests gathered up their belongings, this time preparing for the long trip back to Quebec. Father Garreau made the trip to Etarita to retrieve the bones of Garnier. These relics, like those of de Brébeuf and Lalemant, were wrapped in silk and placed in a chest.

Each day was marked by some progress, but never without the ache of hunger. Canoes were built, more than sixty, to accommodate the fifty Frenchmen and the Hurons. Ragueneau's words revealed his sentiments and those of the priests:

With tears in our eyes we left the country that held our hearts and animated our hopes. Seeing that it had already been bathed in the glorious blood of our brothers, it promised us the same happy lot that would open for us, too, the path to heaven and the gates of paradise. But why complain? We must forget ourselves and leave God for God's sake. I mean that he is worthy of being served for himself alone, without considering our interests.

And on a warm evening in June 1650, men, women, children, the priests, the *donnés*, and the *engagés* boarded the canoes and slipped into the dark waters that would take them away from the second Sainte Marie. As the paddles splashed water into the canoes, Ragueneau looked back in silence and wiped the tears from his face.

After more than ten years of work and untold sacrifices, the Jesuit missions in the Huron country ended. The surviving Hurons found refuge near Quebec, and with the help of the Jesuits, later settled on the Isle of Orleans. The stockade village was called Sainte Marie, but the relentless Iroquois pursued the Hurons even there, and in 1667, the village was abandoned. Eventually a remnant of Hurons established a town still known as L'Ancienne Lorette, later moving this village to La Jeune Lorette on the St. Charles River.

The Hurons ceased to exist as the nation they were at the opening of the missions. Some intermarried with the French or members of the various native tribes, but they continued to follow the Catholic Faith as had been taught to them by Father Jean de Brébeuf and the other missionaries. In 1984, a group of Catholic Hurons, descendants from these early converts, met with Pope John Paul II during his visit to the Midland Shrine in Ontario.

Jesuit efforts to establish Catholic missions and bring the word of God to the native peoples of the New World were abandoned for a time, but the purpose of the Huron missions did not end with the physical destruction of Huronia. The work of the missionaries continued to produce good seed in new ground. As the Jesuits continued to teach and live the Gospel message in the surrounding nations, they found that the Faith had preceded them through Huron captives and refugees. The seed that had been planted and watered with the blood of martyrs, both French and Huron, had taken root and flourished.

APPENDIX

The Martyrs' Shrine in Midland

Huronia was an area of about thirty square miles located in what is now Ontario, Canada. It remained desolate for almost two centuries after the Jesuits abandoned Sainte Marie II. Six priests: Isaac Jogues, Gabriel Lalemant, Jean de Brébeuf, Antoine Daniel, Noël Chabanel, and Charles Garnier, and two *donnés*: Jean de la Lande, and René Goupil had given their lives in their zealous efforts to evangelize the native peoples.

We know from excavations of the original Sainte Marie that in ten years it had expanded into a self-sufficient community, one that became a model of European society. Sainte Marie was the largest inland settlement north of Mexico. It maintained a blacksmith shop, a cookhouse, a bakery, a hospital, living quarters, and a farm that raised a variety of crops and animals. It also had a church named St. Joseph.

Well-protected with three bastions and strong stockade walls, Sainte Marie was a progressive and self-sufficient enterprise. It boasted a system of locks that could move boats or canoes through the canals, and its grainaries and storehouses ensured an abundant supply of food in case of disaster. Here the priests gathered together two or three times a year for

131

fellowship and community. The missioners, except for the superior and his assistants, traveled most of the time to minister to the people in scattered villages.

In the years after the Hurons and the remaining missionaries fled to Quebec in 1650, a handful of Jesuits struggled to evangelize other nations, including the Iroquois. A model among them was the "Lily of the Mohawks," Kateri Tekakwitha, a young woman who lived a life of heroic virtue. Pope John Paul II beatified her in 1980.

Around the mid-nineteenth century, the Jesuit Father Pierre Chazzelle visited the ruins of Sainte Marie, having been inspired by the *Jesuit Relations*. Father Chazzelle's interest in the original site led him to champion the pursuit of excavations. He also hoped to locate St. Ignace.

Later, Father Felix Martin continued Father Chazzelle's interest in the martyrs. Martin was instrumental in petitioning Rome through the Council of Baltimore and the Council of Quebec, requesting the canonization of the eight Jesuits who had been martyred in the New World.

In 1874, Father Laboreau, after exploring a suitable location, built a small chapel to honor the martyrs on a spot he believed had been the site of St. Ignace. A larger church was built later when Father Arthur Jones, a Jesuit historian, studied the letters of the missionaries and confirmed the site as the location of de Brébeuf and Lalemant's martyrdom.

On August 15, 1907, Archbishop Denis O'Connor of Toronto blessed the first shrine to honor the martyrs. The shrine was called "St. Ignatius of the Martyrs"; it was also known as Martyr's Hill. So many pilgrims visited the holy place that it was necessary to build quarters to accommodate the faithful. Many miracles were reported to have taken place at St. Ignatius of the Martyrs.

Excavations in 1930, carried out in Tay Township by Mr. W. J. Wintemberg and Dr. W. Jury, confirmed previous evidence—this was indeed the site of de Brébeuf and Lalemant's martyrdom. But Father M. J. Filion had thought of moving the Shrine of St. Ignatius of the Martyrs to Saint Marie, where the priests had lived and had been buried. The land was not available, but Filion was able to buy land to the east of the remains of Sainte Marie. On June 21, 1925, the eight Jesuits were beatified, and Mass was celebrated near Sainte Marie at an open-air altar. Crowds of people attended. Interest in the North American martyrs began to grow.

In the autumn of 1925, the Jesuits decided to demolish the old shrine on Martyrs' Hill and began to build a new shrine. The new church was made of wood, but later finished in limestone and beautifully decorated. Mother M. Nealis, R.S.C.J., painted and donated the large mural of the martyrs.

The new shrine, the *Martyrs' Shrine,* exhibits a reliquary containing bones of de Brébeuf, Lalemant, and Garnier. Designed and constructed in France, it depicts the martyrs de Brébeuf and Goupil, along with Champlain and a Huron chief. The ivory base is engraved with the names of the martyrs. A map of the Georgian Bay Mission of 1600 accompanies the inscription. De Brébeuf, Lalemant, and Garnier were the only martyrs whose bones were recovered, since the bodies of the others were either burned or lost. On June 29, 1930, Pope Pius XI canonized the eight martyrs.

From the beginning, the new shrine's location offered hostels for pilgrims, and plans were made to expand the accommodations. A rectory was built close to the grotto of Our Lady of Lourdes. In 1927, an outdoor way of the cross was added. The shrine attracted more and more pilgrims, who reported many favors granted through the intercession of the martyrs.

The Jesuits dreamed of owning the property on which the historical Jesuit landmark, Sainte Marie, was situated. This had been the first resting place for the bodies of de Brébeuf and Lalemant. They also hoped that once the land was purchased, the old residence might be restored. The land had been a Huron gift to the Jesuits in 1639, and since that time the property had had many owners.

Through the efforts of Father Tim Lally, director of the shrine, the Jesuits obtained possession of the original Sainte Marie in March 1940. Now more excavations could be made to locate the 1649 gravesites of de Brébeuf and Lalemant. During excavations in 1954, Father Denis Hegarty unearthed a lead coffin plate that read: *Le Père Jean de Brébeuf. Brulé par les Iroquois le 17 mars, l'an 1649.* (Father Jean de Brébeuf. Burned by the Iroquois on March 17, 1649.) Other indications showed that Lalemant's resting place was in the same grave.

In 1964, the Jesuits leased the land for one dollar to the Ontario government. The government agreed to rebuild and reconstruct the historic site, opening it to visitors. The chapel of St. Joseph was restored along with the rest of the mission.

The missionaries called Sainte Marie the "Home of Peace." Here Joseph Chihwatenhwa, the Christian Indian chief, made the spiritual exercises. Today a beautiful statue dedicated to him stands near the shrine church, depicting him with an eagle feather in one hand and a cross in the other.

The twenty-three acre area of the shrine is composed of gardens, pond, and grassy slopes. At the top of a hill near the Stations of the Cross, a covered lookout enables one to see the Wye River as it stretches to Georgian Bay to the north.

The Martyrs' Shrine, Auriesville, New York

Located forty miles west of Albany, New York, in the beautiful Mohawk Valley, the *Martyrs' Shrine* marks the site of the Mohawk village of Ossernenon. Father Isaac Jogues and René Goupil were brought there in August 1642 after their capture, and Goupil was martyred there on September 29, 1642. Jogues buried the body in a nearby ravine, but the remains were never recovered. Jogues met his martyrdom on October 18, 1646, and his companion Jean de la Lande was martyred the next day. Blessed Kateri Tekakwitha, the Mohawk maiden, was born in Ossernenon in 1656, during the time the Jesuits were struggling to evangelize the native peoples.

The *Martyrs' Shrine* began in 1885 as a monument to the North American martyrs. The Coliseum church (a round church), which opened in 1931, can accommodate approximately 6,500 people. The shrine overlooks the Mohawk River and is easily accessible from the New York State Thruway. On the grassy slopes of the grounds, the Stations of the Cross lead to the spot where Jogues and Goupil prayed together. Beautiful statues adorn the surrounding area, including one of Our Lady and Kateri Tekakwitha. Chapels, a Martyrs' Museum, the National Kateri Center, and a large cafeteria are located at the site. Motels are available in nearby cities: Fultonville, Fonda, Amsterdam, Johnstown, and Gloversville, all of which are within three to ten miles of Auriesville. The National Tekakwitha Shrine is four miles from Auriesville, located on Route 5 west of Fonda.

Addresses:

> Martyrs' Shrine
> Midland, Ontario, Canada L4R 4KS
>
> Martyrs' Shrine
> Auriesville, New York 12016

PASTORAL LETTER OF THE CANADIAN BISHOPS FOR THE 350TH ANNIVERSARY OF THE CANADIAN MARTYRS

"Founding Team"

The Church this year celebrates the 350th anniversary of the deaths of those whom we refer to today as the Canadian or North American Martyrs (1649–1999). They were Jesuit Fathers Jean de Brébeuf, Antoine Daniel, Gabriel Lalemant, Charles Garnier, and Noël Chabanel, who died on what is now Canadian soil in the region of Midland, Ontario, together with Father Isaac Jogues and two *donnés* or lay volunteer workers, René Goupil and Jean de la Lande, who died in what is today the United States, in the region of Auriesville, New York.

They are part of that team of "greats" who founded the Church in Canada, which also included Sisters Marie de l'Incarnation, Catherine de Saint-Augustin, Marguerite Bourgeoys and Marguerite d'Youville, Bishop François de Montmorency Laval and the Mohawk ascetic Kateri Tekakwitha.

The 350th anniversary of the Canadian Martyrs draws our attention to an event that inspires and revives Christian fervor. They are for us role models who lived the Gospel ideal to the fullest, leaving a heritage of values that are especially meaningful in our own day.

Beatified in 1925 and then canonized in 1930 by Pius XI, the Canadian Martyrs were proclaimed the secondary patrons of Canada by Pius XII on October 16, 1940—St. Joseph remains our country's primary patron. Commemorated on September 26 in the Canadian liturgical calendar, they are remembered on October 19 in the Church's universal calendar.

The Gospel is intended "for all people of all ages, all conditions, all cultures" (Pope John Paul II). Thus it was, faithful to the Lord's command to "make disciples of all the nations" (Mt 28:19), that these eight missionaries became exiles in order to bring the Gospel to the family of Georgian Bay Amerindians and lead them to holiness. In fifteen years (1634–1649), they transformed the Huron villages there and then what were to become the Quebec villages of Notre Dame-de-Foy and Notre Dame-de-Lorette, making them centers of religious fervor comparable to those in the early Church.

Meeting of cultures

For France, the seventeenth century coincides with its great projects of exploration, resulting in the foundation of Quebec in 1608, and the creation of the Company of One Hundred Associates under Cardinal Richelieu in 1627. The Company's mandate was threefold: to encourage settlement, commercial development, and evangelization. However, the mandate also presented certain ambiguities, since it risked portraying the missionaries as political precursors or even agents. By being allied with France and its projects, the missionaries found themselves in the middle of a game of commercial competition being played out by Dutch, English and French, as well as caught in hostilities between the Hurons and Iroquois. Living on such dangerous ground and in a highly explosive atmosphere, it was a context in which they could not escape the risk of one day becoming victims in what was a tragic game of rivalries.

The missionaries had only one option: openly declaring their plans to evangelize and dissociating themselves from the commercial goals of the European nations. This is exactly what de Brébeuf did upon his arrival in Huron territory in 1634: "Seeing them all together [the Hurons], we determined to preach publicly and make known to them the reason for coming to their country, not for their furs but to proclaim to them the true God and his Son, Jesus Christ, the one Savior of our souls" (*Jesuit Relations: Relation* of Paul Le Jeune, 1635, chapter on de Brébeuf). Until 1650, the missionaries accordingly refused to welcome merchants, hustlers and the fur traders known as the *coureurs de bois*.

Evangelization, however, presented even greater problems than did the political situation. The missionaries were European and French, and so they found themselves confronted by a completely new culture. They would have only fifteen years to decipher the Huron language and to unlock what were to them the even more impenetrable mysteries presented by the customs of the land. In order to be perceived as Huron in the eyes of the Hurons, they adopted Huron ways of living and eating. They never once tried making the Hurons French. Instead, they created a written language for them, which had not existed before—a language with no affinity to European languages and which took the Jesuits no less than six to eight years to learn. They became *inculturated* long before the term existed.

Their most difficult challenge was trying to understand Amerindian customs. On this front, the missionaries struggled blindly, yet admitted their limitations and mistakes while also correcting their judgments. Each day they came to understand those customs a little more, as indicated by Fr. Paul Ragueneau, third superior of the mission: "One must be very careful before condemning a thousand things among their customs, which greatly offend minds nurtured and set in another world.... I have no hesitation in saying that we have been too severe on this point.... We see that such severity is no longer necessary and that in many things we can be less rigorous than in the past" (*Relation* of Paul Ragueneau, 1648–1649).

Amazingly, these European missionaries came to such discernment after only fifteen years—which is impressive even in our own time. What is surprising is not what they failed to understand, but all that they understood in so short a time.

Huron mission

At the beginning of the seventeenth century, the Society of Jesus was expanding throughout France. The canonization in 1622 of Francis Xavier, the apostle of the Indies, captured the imagination of young Jesuits and their students. A great missionary frenzy swept through the country.

Permeating colleges, filling both soul and sails, it transported hearts and minds to far away lands and other populations waiting to be evangelized—especially to New France where colonization had just begun. Like a fire so whipped by the wind it was able to jump across the waters, the zeal of young French religious could not be contained.

Thus it was, from 1634 to 1649, about thirty Jesuits, twenty of whom were priests, exiled themselves to preach the Gospel on the shores of Lake Huron. This mission, the largest of all the Jesuit missions in North America, was also one of the most difficult in the history of the Society of Jesus. The missionaries encountered what to them were appalling conditions, including climate, food, and shelter. Finding themselves in a country of enormous proportions, they covered distances of many hundred kilometers in fragile bark canoes, through waterfalls and rapids, afflicted by the scourge of mosquitoes, the difficulties of getting fresh supplies and the fatigue of trekking through the wilderness.

At first, they experienced the comforting friendship of those they had come to evangelize. Then the missionaries began to encounter growing resistance. Part of the explanation was a series of epidemics for which they were blamed, but there was also the disparity between the Gospel and certain customs of the land. From 1636 to 1641, the mission lived in an atmosphere of distrust, persecution, and even death threats. As of 1641, there were only sixty Christians. De Brébeuf waited six years before he was able to baptize one healthy adult. However, with several influential leaders eventually accepting the Gospel, the missionary work was able to move forward step by step. By 1649, at the time of the last Iroquois offensive against the Hurons, the majority of the Huron Nation had become Christian. It should also be noted here that conversion meant a transition to a heroic Christian life. The missionaries were convinced that the Hurons, like any other people, were capable of reaching the heights of humanity attained by saints.

Supreme expression of love

The missionaries of Huronia could not accept mediocrity. Their sole option was to be heroic or quit—which some did. But the majority of them were driven by a burning zeal. When Jerome Lalemant, the second superior of Huronia, had just arrived from France, he said the reason there were still so few Christians in Huronia at that time was that there had not yet been any martyrs. He was obliged to change his opinion. The truth is that the missionaries were full-time martyrs. As he was later to say, most people would have preferred to "be hit suddenly over the head by a hatchet blow than live through years of the life which we must lead here every day" (*Relation* of Paul Le Jeune, 1639, chapter on Jerome Lalemant). Living only for Christ, continuously contemplating him, in the end they resembled the Lord.

Their consuming martyrdom involved no less than completely surrendering their lives in the ultimate offering. For too long now Christian martyrdom has been talked about in terms of torture, execution, and hatred of the faith, which completely misrepresents what is most profound about it. The Second Vatican Council made an important distinction in this regard. It taught that martyrs follow in the footsteps of Jesus to the point of making even their death a gift to Christ thereby attesting that salvation comes from the Lord and the Gospel. As the *Constitution on the Church* states:

"Since Jesus, the Son of God, manifested his love by laying down his life for us, no one has greater love than they who lay down their lives for Christ and for their sisters and brothers (see 1 Jn 3:16; Jn 15:13).... Martyrdom makes the disciples like their master, who willingly accepted death for the salvation of the world, and through it they are made like him by the shedding of blood. Therefore, the Church considers it the highest gift and the supreme test of love" (*Lumen Gentium*, n. 42).

The Second Vatican Council did not refer to hatred of the faith. Instead, the determining criteria for martyrdom are positive: giving one's life for Christ and for one's brothers and sisters out of overwhelming love. It is not the executioner, the persecutor, or the historian who declares someone a martyr. It is a decision that the Church makes on the basis of what motivated the martyred person. Thus, we cannot separate the death of the missionaries in Huronia from the meaning it had for them. In dying for us, Jesus is not put to death, but chooses to lay down his life for us.

In this light, we see that the missionaries of Huronia are martyrs for two reasons: because of their faith, and above all because they witnessed to the love they had for the Native Peoples for whose sake they gave up their lives, following in the footsteps of Jesus. In proclaiming Christ and the Gospel, they were fully aware they risked death, as they clearly stated on a number of occasions.

Heritage of values

At a time when many Christian values are at odds with our society, the heritage of the Canadian Martyrs is even more evident. Their values can help us all in repairing the spiritual fabric of our Church and society, just as their spirit of self-sacrifice and openness to others challenges each of us. Let us recall a few of the traits at work in their lives.

Most importantly, they had an intense devotion to Christ. This was the principle on which they based their entire existence. For them, Christ was a living presence who was always with them—in their travels, ministry, suffering, and martyrdom. Like St. Paul, they had been captured by Christ (Phil 3:12). For the Hurons, the missionaries were a visible expression of Christ, loving them even to the point of dying for them.

This devotion to Christ explains the zeal that burned more intensely than the fires that eventually consumed them. It was this zeal that inspired de Brébeuf to make the following astounding statement: "My God, would that you were better known! Would that this whole Native People have converted itself completely to you! How you are loved! Yes, my God, if all of the torment endured by the captives of this land...should fall upon me, I would offer myself to them with all my heart and I alone would suffer them!" (*Relation* of Paul Ragueneau, 1648–49). It took twenty such missionaries to bring the Gospel to an entire nation and raise its people to the heights of holiness. Do we today have just a little of this same zeal for what is needed in a new evangelization?

It was this zeal that made the Huron missionaries so perceptive in understanding all that inculturation must involve— adopting Amerindian ways of living and eating, and using Huron language and symbols in paintings and images for teaching and catechizing.

As well, they were wonderfully generous in their daily relationships with one another. Each would praise other co-workers while refusing any kind of special favor for himself.

Finally, they had an astonishing spirit of prayer. Here we see evidence of a mysterious inner life filled with divine power and grace. De Brébeuf said, "God gave us the day for dealing with our neighbor and nighttime for conversing with the Lord" (*Relation* of Paul Ragueneau, 1648–49). Contemplative even in their actions, they saw God present everywhere.

Although the Jesuit mission in Huronia disappeared with the martyrdom of its founders, the dispersal of the Hurons after 1650 resulted in the spreading of the Gospel throughout the region of the Great Lakes and along the Hudson River. Those who had been converted became the core of a Christian presence both among the Iroquois and among aboriginal nations more to the west. Thus, through the Huron Christians and the blood of the Jesuit martyrs, the faith was kindled throughout North America.

We thank God for giving the Church in Canada such impressive founders and models. As we begin the new millennium and find ourselves challenged to undertake a new evangelization, we are encouraged by the witness of the Canadian Martyrs and their devotion to Christ, as well as by their courageous zeal and spirit of prayer. Fortunately, their memory is also kept alive in a special way at the Martyrs' Shrine in Midland, Ontario—the scene for a significant part of their mission work and which is located in the general region where five of them actually died. For those of us who can, a pilgrimage there will be an important way of marking this 350th anniversary and rediscovering our spiritual heritage.

Feast of the Triumph of the Cross, September 14, 1999

BIBLIOGRAPHY

Beauchamp, William M. *A History of the New York Iroquois.* New York: Ira J. Friedman, Inc., 1962.

Campbell, Thomas Joseph. *Isaac Jogues.* New York: American Press, 1911.

Catlin, George. *North American Indians.* 2 vols. London: 1841.

Donnelly, Joseph P. *Jean de Brébeuf.* Chicago: Loyola University Press, 1975.

Fallon, Rev. J., S.J. *Shadows Over Huronia: The Jesuit Relations.* Midland, Ontario: The Martyrs' Shrine, 1965.

Hollis, Christopher. *The Jesuits: A History.* New York: Macmillan Press, 1968.

LaFarge, J. *A Report on the American Jesuits.* New York: Farrar, Straus and Cudahy, 1956.

Leland, Charles G. *The Algonquin Legends of New England.* Boston: Houghton, Mifflin and Company, 1884.

Miller, Rene Fulop. *The Jesuits: A History of the Society of Jesus.* New York: Capricorn Books, 1963.

Morgan, Lewis H. *League of the Iroquois.* 2 vols. New York: Burt Franklin, 1901.

Owen, Deetz, Fisher. *The North American Indians: A Sourcebook*. New York: Macmillan Company, 1965.

O'Brien, John A. *The American Martyrs: The Story of the Eight Jesuit Martyrs of North America*. New York: Appleton-Century-Crofts, Inc., 1953.

Parker, Gilbert and Claude G. Bryan. *Old Quebec: the Fortress of New France*. London: The Macmillan Company, 1903.

Parkman, Francis. *The Jesuits of North America*. Boston: Little, Brown & Company, 1963.

Roustang, Francois, S.J., ed. *An Autobiography of Martyrdom: Spiritual Writings of the Jesuits in New France*. St. Louis, MO: B. Herder Book Co., 1964.

Talbot, Francis, S.J. *Saint Among Savages: The Life of Isaac Jogues*. New York: Harper and Brothers, 1935.

Talbot, Francis, S.J. *Saint Among the Hurons: The Life of Jean de Brébeuf*. New York: Harper and Brothers, 1949.

*Thwaites, Reuben Gold, ed. *The Jesuit Relations and Allied Documents*, 73 vols. Cleveland: The Burrows Brothers Company, 1896–1901.

Vecsey, Christopher. *The Paths of Kateri's Kin*. Notre Dame, IN: University of Notre Dame Press, 1997.

Wynne, John, S.J. *The Jesuit Martyrs of North America*. New York: Universal Knowledge Foundation, 1925.

* This is the most significant of all the sources.

Pauline
BOOKS & MEDIA

The Daughters of St. Paul operate book and media centers at the following addresses. Visit, call or write the one nearest you today, or find us on the World Wide Web, www.pauline.org

CALIFORNIA
3908 Sepulveda Blvd, Culver City, CA 90230   310-397-8676
5945 Balboa Avenue, San Diego, CA 92111   858-565-9181
46 Geary Street, San Francisco, CA 94108   415-781-5180

FLORIDA
145 S.W. 107th Avenue, Miami, FL 33174   305-559-6715

HAWAII
1143 Bishop Street, Honolulu, HI 96813   808-521-2731
Neighbor Islands call: 800-259-8463

ILLINOIS
172 North Michigan Avenue, Chicago, IL 60601   312-346-4228

LOUISIANA
4403 Veterans Memorial Blvd, Metairie, LA 70006   504-887-7631

MASSACHUSETTS
Rte. 1, 885 Providence Hwy, Dedham, MA 02026   781-326-5385

MISSOURI
9804 Watson Road, St. Louis, MO 63126   314-965-3512

NEW JERSEY
561 U.S. Route 1, Wick Plaza, Edison, NJ 08817   732-572-1200

NEW YORK
150 East 52nd Street, New York, NY 10022   212-754-1110
78 Fort Place, Staten Island, NY 10301   718-447-5071

OHIO
2105 Ontario Street, Cleveland, OH 44115   216-621-9427

PENNSYLVANIA
9171-A Roosevelt Blvd, Philadelphia, PA 19114   215-676-9494

SOUTH CAROLINA
243 King Street, Charleston, SC 29401   843-577-0175

TENNESSEE
4811 Poplar Avenue, Memphis, TN 38117   901-761-2987

TEXAS
114 Main Plaza, San Antonio, TX 78205   210-224-8101

VIRGINIA
1025 King Street, Alexandria, VA 22314   703-549-3806

CANADA
3022 Dufferin Street, Toronto, Ontario, Canada M6B 3T5   416-781-9131
1155 Yonge Street, Toronto, Ontario, Canada M4T 1W2   416-934-3440

¡También somos su fuente para libros, videos y música en español!